Paul Manning was a Cam[...]
National Trust member until [...]
Smell of Brut. A brief caree[...]
and novelty luggage tag salesman led swiftly to a two
week engagement as compere of T.V.'s spectacular
Saturday Night at The Moon and Parrot. He became
a full time writer in 1954, having answered an
advertisement in the personal columns of the
Exchange and Mart. His many novels, films and
plays include: *Sons and Wallies*, *Escape from Milton
Keynes*, *Funeral in Welwyn Garden City* and the
smash hit musical *Hello Wally!* which enjoyed a
record-breaking four day run at the Streatham
Hippodrome. He is currently writing a sequel to *How
To Be a Wally*, entitled *How To Be A Complete and
Utter Wally*, soon to be available in a luxuriously
tooled twenty-two volume edition and a Wally's
Digest Condensed Video.

To: Walter

Merry Christmas 1984

In one sense you don't need this book but, in another sense you're going to need all the help you can get to be a sucessful Wally! Have fun trying!

Jolann and Patrick

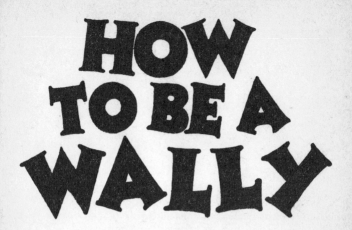

HOW TO BE A WALLY

PAUL MANNING

A Moon and Parrot Publication from

Futura

A Futura BOOK

First published in 1983
by Futura Publications, a Divison of
Macdonald & Co. (Publishers) Ltd.
London & Sydney
Reprinted 1983 (three times), 1984 (twice)

ISBN 0 7088 2440 4

Photoset in North Wales by
Derek Doyle & Associates, Mold, Clwyd
Printed in Great Britain by
Hazell Watson & Viney Limited,
Member of the BPCC Group,
Aylesbury, Bucks

Futura Publications
A Division of
Macdonald & Co (Publishers) Ltd
Maxwell House
74 Worship Street
London EC2A 2EN
A BPCC plc Company

CONTENTS

INTRODUCTION

History affords many examples of famous men and women who narrowly missed being Wallies.

Sir Francis Drake, for instance, could so easily have been a Wally if instead of playing bowls on Plymouth Hoe, he'd been playing Crazy Golf.

Boadicea could have had the honour of being history's first female Wally if instead of fitting blades to the wheels of her chariot, she'd stencilled her name on the front or decorated it with a couple of fluffy dice.

King John could have been a Wally if he'd signed Magna Carta with a giant novelty biro. So could King Arthur, if he'd covered the Round Table with woodgrain laminate.

Nero, too, missed a golden opportunity to be a Wally by fiddling while Rome burned instead of playing a medley from *Evita* on the Hammond Organ.

Of them all, perhaps King Alfred came the closest to being a Wally when he burnt the cakes. He wasn't to know that Wallies don't cook their own – they prefer Mr Kipling's Coffee Gateaux from the local Spar shop.

They and many more like them were all unlucky. They didn't know the form. They Got It Wrong.

You on the other hand are more fortunate. Thanks to this book you can learn all you need to know in order to become a Wally. With practice, patience and application you can avoid their mistakes and Get It Right, if not first time, then at least on your twentieth or possibly thirtieth try.

But first, what exactly *is* a Wally?

A Wally, for the benefit of those few benighted souls who don't already know, is someone who keeps the current issue of the *TV Times* in an embossed imitation leather binder. He drives a customised Ford Cortina with his name stencilled on the windscreen alongside that of his girlfriend, Go Faster stripes on the sides, and probably a sticker on the back that says 'My Other Car's a Porsche'. At heavy metal concerts you'll find scores of apprentice Wallies, but the real hard-core Wallies are easy to spot: they're the ones bobbing up and down at the back, playing imaginary guitars.

Many Wallies are also headbangers, but it doesn't necessarily follow. All headbangers, however, are by definition Wallies.

The person who sabotaged your office vending machine by gumming up the works with foreign coins was probably a Wally. Those people you see waving scarves and fluffy toys and grinning inanely at you from the back of coaches are *definitely* Wallies. The person who tries to sell you double-glazing and tells you he's installed it in his own home is a Wally. If you believe him, you're one too – and you don't need any help from this book after all.

A Wally is someone who has a sticker on his steering wheel saying 'Belt Up – Be a Life-saver' – and still forgets to wear a seatbelt. His idea of gardening is to buy a roll of nylon lawn, lay it in his back garden, attempt to mow it with a Flymo and accidentally slice through the flex. He has been known to shave his chest hair in order to stimulate the growth.

Being a Wally is a doddle – a piece of cake. Right?

Wrong. It's time this idea was knocked firmly on the head. Being a Wally is *not* just a question of swanning around in an acrylic sweater, wearing Brut, or taking the occasional joy-ride in a supermarket trolley. It *is* all these things, but it's also a great deal more. It can mean standing outside D.E.R. showrooms in the pouring rain watching 'Game For A Laugh'. Or boldly forsaking the safety of a car in Safari parks in order to offer prawn cocktail-flavoured crisps to the lions. Or braving carbon monoxide poisoning by picnicking within inches of passing juggernauts. Or riding three at a time on coin-operated rocking horses in C & A. Often it involves risking life and limb. In some cases your own.

Above all, being a Wally is a state of mind. It's writing glowing testimonials in the visitors' book of a Little Chef – and meaning every word of it. It's not being able to work out the right-of-way system at mini-roundabouts. It's preferring Coffeemate to milk. It's being genuinely unable to tell Stork from butter, and proud of it.

Today's highly-skilled all-round Wally makes all this seem deceptively simple. How many times have you

8

watched Wallies holding arm-wrestling matches in Inter-City buffet cars or spraying each other with Fanta in suburban shopping precincts and thought to yourself: *I could do that?* The trouble is, it may look effortless but in actual fact being a Wally takes long hours of practice, grit and determination, and a great deal of patience and understanding on the part of your family and friends. Yes: it's a long hard slog before you earn the right to wear the coveted order of the Sick Parrot.

Take Wally home decor, for instance. As every Wally knows, a lounge is a room containing a cosily glowing log-effect gas fire with imitation brass fire tongs, and a bar strung with fairy lights and decked out in sumptuous black crackle vinyl; it also usually contains a glass-fronted bookcase containing classics of world literature bound in handsome hand-tooled vellum and printed on toilet paper, plus a mysterious green-glowing object containing slowly drifting chunks of ectoplasm.

But how does a Wally know that this is the correct, indeed the *only*, way to adorn his home? After all, there are very few magazines to point him in the right direction – no *Ideal Wally* with full-colour spreads of Wallies sprawled casually on orange nylon hearth-rugs or leatherette settees watching Celebrity Snooker; no helpful colour supplement articles listing stockists of Wally accoutrements. So how does he do it?

The answer's simple: flair. Whereas a novice such as yourself might be tempted to introduce a touch of stripped pine or a Hockney print and ruin the whole effect, the experienced Wally never puts a foot wrong. Whether he's decorating his home or arranging postcards, novelties or executive desk toys at his place of work, the real Wally Gets It Right.

Of course, in the early stages you can't hope to match that kind of prowess. But there are obvious bloomers that you can avoid with the help of this book. Embarrassing slips of the tongue, like saying 'I couldn't agree more' instead of 'This is it', or announcing that you're 'delighted', or 'thrilled' when you should be 'over the moon'. Social *faux-pas*, like putting an empty crisp packet straight into a litter bin instead of blowing it up and bursting it; opening a can of lager and forgetting to give it a good shake first so that you can direct a jet of froth over your fellow-Wallies; throwing up in the bathroom at parties, unaware that the correct place is the kitchen sink: they're little things; but they can mark the difference between being a Complete Wally and just A Bit of A Wally – and let's face it, if you're only going to be A Bit Of A Wally, you might just as well save yourself the trouble and not be a Wally at all.

It's tough to have to say this, but one thing this book will teach you is that not everybody can be a Wally. One has to be brutally realistic about this. Some people, such as High Court Judges and Buddhists, will never be Wallies in a million years – except in very unusual circumstances (see p. 34). Maybe they were deprived of the right kind of stimulus in early childhood – the Yorkie bars, the chance to browse through Mum's Barry Manilow albums, watch Breakfast Television, or flip through Dad's week-by-week pictorial encyclopedia of the War In The Falklands. Maybe when other kids were out posting empty Kentucky Fried Chicken boxes through old ladies' letterboxes they preferred to sit at home glued to the Open University. Maybe their parents were never prepared to make the sacrifices or give them the breaks. Who knows? Maybe they just didn't have it in them from the start.

That's the bad news.

The *good* news is that in spite of all that, Wallies are definitely on the increase. Look around you. You can probably think of several 'occasional' Wallies and at least one dedicated full-timer in your immediate circle of acquaintance. Time was when there was one in every office. Now there's more likely to be a whole gang of them, who come roaring back from the Moon and Parrot after lunch and spend the entire afternoon pinching bottoms, chucking darts at *Playboy* centrefolds and flicking rubber bands at each other.

There are other pointers to this massive upsurge in the Wally population. In the past it was not uncommon to see the odd pair or handful of Wallies gamely getting plastered on duty-free booze and lurching drunkenly around the passenger lounges on board cross-Channel ferries. Nowadays they're coming out of the portholes. In fact, so many Wallies seem willing to part with hard cash for a chance to throw up in the English Channel that the more far-sighted ferry operators have even laid on special day trips for this very purpose.

Today Wallies can be found in all walks of life: in schools, technical colleges, the nationalised industries (particularly on the customer relations side, where their social and interpersonal skills can be exploited to the full), factories, offices, government departments — even universities. Indeed, there's growing evidence that our institutions of higher education are turning them out in ever-increasing numbers.

Oxford and Cambridge, to be fair, have been creating a goodly proportion of the nation's Wallies over the past few centuries. However, until recently their intake was limited to sons of clergymen, Wallies with pots of money, blue-blooded Wallies stunted by generations of in-breeding, or Wallies with some kind of sporting prowess. Happily, this kind of elitism is now a thing of the past; taking their lead from other more forward-looking universities, Oxford and Cambridge have started opening their doors to Wallies from all strata of society.

There are also signs that after a slow start the Wally phenomenon is beginning to catch on abroad. At the risk of sounding a bit chauvinistic, this is largely due to the selfless missionary zeal of hordes of invading British Wallies who, while on holiday or attending international sporting fixtures, have taken the opportunity to show the continentals how it's done — often receiving for their pains harsh treatment from armies of uniformed killjoys and jackbooted petty bureaucrats. Many British Wallies have even had to suffer fines and imprisonment at the hands of narrow-minded continental officialdom — usually for so-called 'crimes' no more serious than the wrecking of football stadiums, the wholesale looting of shops and the burning down of hotels.

Luckily this doesn't seem to have dampened their spirits. Quite the reverse: it's made them all the more determined to go back and have another bash next year.

This book and how to use it

How to be a Wally is intended primarily for you, the would-be male Wally. This isn't through any deep or ingrained chauvinist bias on the part of the author. It's just that by general agreement most Wallies are male, so it seems reasonable to suppose that most aspiring Wallies will be male too.

There are of course many female Wallies with habits of speech, dress and behaviour all their own (see p. 26); but sex equality has been lamentably slow in reaching the Wally world and the range of activities open to Wally women is still limited. The female Wally's traditional role is simply to supply a name to be stencilled on to your car windscreen, to occupy the passenger seat, to sip expensive and brightly coloured drinks with cherries and parasols bobbing around on the top, to send matinee jackets to Prince William and embroidered Valentine cards to Richard Clayderman, and generally to act as amused and admiring spectator while you get on with the more important and worthwhile tasks assigned to the male Wally. It's not much of a life for her, but there it is. Don't take her for granted. Remember: she may not be able to demonstrate that she's a Wally by roaring down inland waterways in power-boats or smashing up grand pianos — although there's nothing to stop her having a go — but she more than proves she's a Wally by putting up with you.

But what of the contents of this book? What will it teach you that you couldn't work out for yourself?

Well, the first and most obvious point is that whatever your age and physical appearance, you'll need to get into the habit of thinking, acting and looking like a Wally – and that means close attention to detail. It means *not* putting your foot in it by committing breaches of Wally etiquette, by using the wrong words or phrases, for instance, or carelessly removing the aforementioned classics of world literature from their glass-fronted cabinet and attempting to read them. It means, in short, achieving Wally credibility. So a general section first, which should be read carefully by *all* would-be Wallies.

Secondly, there are a number of Wally skills which can only be acquired with the help of expert guidance: the correct way to drink from a ring-pull can; the correct way to play the imaginary guitar at Status Quo concerts, working in all the approved facial contortions; the correct way to transform the exterior of your home. This book will help you master them all with the aid of simple step-by-step diagrams that not even the most accomplished Wally could fail to grasp.

How to be a Wally also contains major sections covering all the key areas of Wally activity. There's a Wallies on Wheels section, explaining amongst other things the rather special requirements of the Wally Highway Code, and telling you how to get the best out of your Colonel Bogey Car Horn. There's a Wally Consumer Guide explaining how to shop like a Wally. A Wally food and drink guide. A home furnishing guide. A holidaymaker's guide. A guide to the pleasures of supermarket trolley cruising, roadside picnicking, and sweltering in mile-long queues of holiday traffic. Lastly, there's a tear-off membership form for the All-England Wally Club, a non-profitmaking organisation dedicated to serving the interests of Wallies, whose recent activities have included sponsored bollard-leaping (all proceeds go to cover the cost of subsequent hospital treatment) and a highly successful competition in which entrants had to guess to the nearest yard Barry Manilow's inside leg measurement.

13

How to be a Wally is written in short, fairly manageable sections and doesn't contain too many long words, but if you do find it's all getting a bit much for you, just put it on one side for a few moments and lie down with a cold flannel over your head until your brain's had a chance to recover. Then you can come back to it afresh.

GET IT RIGHT

How to achieve Wally credibility

In order to be a true Wally you must have Wally credibility. This means not only being a Wally, but showing the scars to prove it.

There are various immediately recognisable signs of Wally credibility. A leg or arm in plaster, for instance, gives Wally credibility – particularly if the plaster has been signed by all your Wally friends. An inverted coat hanger in place of an aerial on your car can give Wally credibility, and so can fibreglass patches on the bodywork, suggesting hours of toil in the garage. Any wounds or injuries received in the course of DIY projects give Wally credibility: fingers missing; lacerations caused by careless use of a Black and Decker sanding disc. The same applies to love bites and tattoos.

If you have the right kind of Wally credibility – the kind that comes from knocks and bruises sustained in the hard school of life – you'll be confident and secure enough not to feel you have to make a great song and dance about these things. They'll be part of you. You'll be content to let people notice them and draw their own conclusions. When a friend reminds you admiringly how one New Year's Eve you scaled Nelson's Column and sprayed 'Hissing Sid is innocent' all over it with an aerosol, you'll simply shrug modestly and say, 'It was nothing ... ' This won't be false modesty on your part: just an honest recognition that what you did was neither more nor less than your *duty* as a Wally.

Certain possessions can act as Wally credibility boosters: a darts trophy on the mantelpiece; a plastic motorway cone or stolen lifebelt on top of the wardrobe; a beer tankard with the owner's name engraved on it hanging behind the bar at the Moon and Parrot. All these things discreetly declare to friends and acquaintances that whoever owns them is a Wally.

Naturally, as a beginner, you want to know how to get

hold of these vital pieces of equipment without going through the gruelling apprenticeship your more accomplished fellow-Wallies have already survived.

Unfortunately, it can't be done. There *are* no short cuts. Wally credibility has to be earned. The most that you can hope for is to avoid needlessly blowing your credibility by some elementary blunder. And that's where this section *can* help.

Here then are a few tips to start off with:

1) In order not to blow your Wally credibility you must remember that sports kit must be spotlessly laundered and overalls must be covered with filthy and unmentionable stains – *never* the other way round.
2) Your score on the Space Invaders should either be astronomically high (suggesting that you practise every minute of the day) or pitifully low (suggesting that you will never be any good at it no matter how much you practise) – *never* merely middling or respectable.
3) If you are unfortunate enough to possess a clean driving licence, *never* produce it in the company of your fellow-Wallies.
4) *On no account* leave Penguin Classics on the rear window ledge of your car (or as you should learn to call it, 'motor') alongside the nodding dogs and fluffy dice. This could damage your Wally credibility so seriously that you might never regain your friends' esteem – not even by showing that you can remember the words of an entire Bucks Fizz number and can perform the dance steps too.

Wally Etiquette

Another way to blow your Wally credibility is to commit some unwitting breach of Wally Etiquette. Wally Etiquette consists of the following crucial points:

1) When travelling on the tube, you will entertain other passengers by swinging from the straps like a monkey, chasing other Wallies up and down the carriage, and needlessly obstructing the doors with your foot.

2) When entering a building via swing doors, always go round at least twice and before exiting, give them a hefty push so that anyone still left inside gets their arms and legs crushed.

3) When travelling on a main-line train, it is essential to sit in the luggage rack, scratch your initials on the mirrors, and when leaving, open the door and spring out before the train has stopped moving.

4) On noticing a television interview being conducted outside a football ground or in a shopping centre, be sure either to loiter inanely in the middle distance or to crowd around with a group of other Wallies, pulling funny faces, shouting 'Hello, Mum' and giving thumbs-up signs to the camera.

5) In restaurants, always address the waiter as 'John' and show your appreciation of a really first-class Chicken Vindaloo by swilling it down with at least three pints of Black Label and regurgitating the lot on the pavement outside.

6) Do not smoke between courses. Try and keep a fag on the go throughout the meal.

7) When forced to tell a bare-faced lie, always preface it with the words, 'I'll be honest with you'.

8) On finishing a packet of crisps in a pub, do not forget to blow it up and burst it, showering people with the leftover bits at the bottom of the bag and causing them to spill their drinks.

9) After giving vent to a stream of four-letter words, always ask your listeners to pardon your French.

18

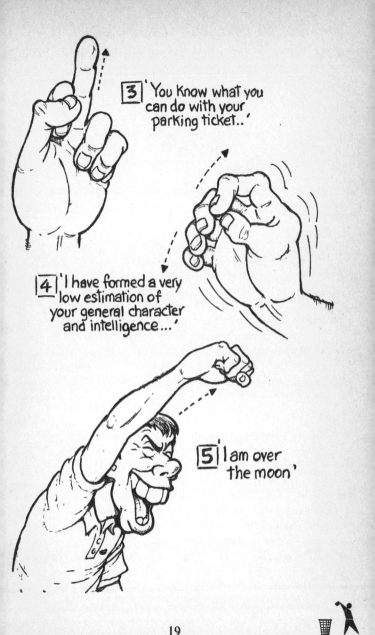

How to talk like a Wally

There's no quicker or easier way to lose what little Wally credibility you have in these crucial early stages than to let slip the wrong word or phrase. How many would-be-Wally shop assistants, for instance, have seen all their hopes dashed simply because they greeted customers with the words 'Can I help you?' instead of the more correct, 'What can I do you for?' To avoid Batemanesque scenes, observe the following rules:

1) On colliding with a police patrol car while practising your emergency stops in a busy suburban high street, express surprise by saying 'Strike a light'. *Not* 'Good heavens'.

2) On winning a huge cash prize in a Reader's Digest Lucky Numbers Draw, you are 'over the moon'. You are *not* 'delighted'.

3) On failing to be selected for the office table football squad, or being given the elbow by your girl-friend and having to go to all the trouble of peeling her name off your windscreen, you are 'sick as a parrot'. You are *not* 'annoyed', 'browned off'.

4) To express agreement with a proposition, *don't* nod or say 'absolutely'. Say, 'this is it'. *E.g*: Wally A: 'You win some, you lose some.' Wally B: 'This is it.'

5) Your Saturday-morning shopping expeditions to Mothercare with the wife are *not* 'a bore'. They are 'a pain in the bum/arse/behind'.

6) The correct response to a joke or amusing remark is 'Like it, like it'. *Not* 'How priceless'.

7) A person who OD's on Ritz Crackers and Sun Pat Blue Cheese Spread is *not* 'a greedy pig', he's a 'gannet'.

8) Your two-week wreck-a-hotel-room-in-all-the-historic-cities-of-Europe coach tour was *not* 'wonderful' or 'marvellous', it was 'magic'.

9) Lastly, in the unlikely event of your finding yourself suddenly thrust into the limelight and asked to make a statement to the news media, do not miss an opportunity to use the words, 'at this moment in time', 'hopefully',

'across the board', 'meaningful dialogue', and to refer at some point to money either 'up front' or 'on the table'.

The following phrases should be banished from your repertoire:
'Within reasonable bounds'
'Off the beaten track'
'A select gathering'
(See also Body Language, pp. 18-19)

Thinking like a Wally

To achieve Wally credibility you must learn to think like a Wally –
– and that means first of all understanding the term *nous*.

Nous is what Wallies have instead of common sense. It's that breezy savoir-faire that enables you to hop without any apparent effort out of one fine mess and straight into another even finer one. It means, for example, knowing short cuts through labyrinthine housing estates that end up by being twice as long as your original route. It also means having at your disposal a vast range of sophisticated labour-saving power-tool attachments in a garage or shack at the bottom of the garden that either fall to pieces or turn out to be lacking some vital component on the one occasion you want to use them. Although nous embraces a number of useful skills – knowing which foreign coins you can use in vending machines or parking meters; how to wind back the clock of your motor; how to bypass gas and electricity meters – it's also to do with *who* you know. It's knowing someone who knows someone else who just might be able to lay his hands on a visor-louvre for the rear window of your Capri – for a price.

Lack of nous can be a handicap for you as an aspiring Wally. In your early shots at DIY, for example, you'll probably muddle along as best you can, putting your foot through walls, burying yourself under piles of plaster dust and masonry and generally being a Bit Of A Wally.

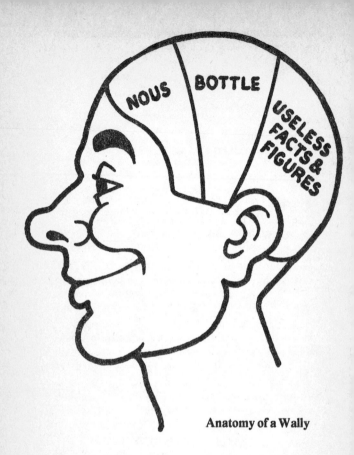

Anatomy of a Wally

If you had a bit more nous, though, you'd have contacts in the trade – cowboys who'd wreak far greater chaos *and* charge you large sums of money for their services. All you'd then have to do is pay them and you'd be right up there among the Complete Wallies.

Unfortunately for you, nous can't be taught in a book. It's something you pick up gradually in the course of being a Wally and mingling with other Wallies. It's made easier

- Nothing beats the great smell of Brut
- Love means never having to say you're sorry
- 99 per cent of all Wallies are caused by accidents
- Every cloud has a sumptuous Wallytex lining
- If you can't stand the heat, get out of the Solarium
- The best things in life are 20p off
- If you can't beat them, try taking up Kung Fu
- Never mind the content, admire the hand-tooled binding
- You can't make a silk purse out of a sow's ear – but you *can* use it to make a very attractive novelty luggage tag.

for you, though, by the fact that they will volunteer, or try to foist, their nous on you whether you're interested or not. When you've acquired it, you can then foist it on other people. You will be able, for instance, to pull in at the roadside when you see a motorist in difficulties, confidently set about taking his engine to bits, still not locate the fault, then find that you can't get the bits back in the right order — at which point you drive off, leaving him considerably worse off than before you arrived.

Bottle is another vital quality for any Wally. It can be defined roughly as: valour minus discretion.

Most Wally activities call for bottle, some more than others. Ordering 'Spling Lolls' in a Chinese Take-Away requires relatively little. Late-night shopping at Key Markets or battling your way up the down escalator during the rush hour require rather more. Striding into a para-troopers' mess and announcing that you thought only fairies had wings requires a great deal.

Whatever activity you're engaged in, the important thing is not to lose your bottle or 'bottle out' halfway through. For instance, when a policeman stops you for speeding the wrong way down a one-way street and asks, 'Didn't you see the arrows?', you should reply promptly, 'Arrows, John? I didn't even see the Indians.' If you simply shrug your shoulders, grin vacantly and mutter something about it being a fair cop, you'll lose valuable Wally credibility points; in fact, you won't be a Wally at all, you'll be a Turkey.

Before concluding this short section on how to think like a Wally, some mention should be made of the contents of your data banks. Do not confuse being a Wally with being an ignoramus. An ignoramus is empty-headed, whereas your head should be sufficiently well-stocked with facts and figures to enable you at least to answer questions on local radio phone-ins and to stand a reasonable chance of winning the latest Duran Duran single or a Return of the Jedi T-shirt — and if possible to score respectably on The Pop Quiz and A Question of Sport as well. Not by actually taking part in the programmes of course, but by shouting out the answers as you watch at home, or even better, as you stand mesmerised in front of banks of television screens in the electrical goods department of Debenham's.

In addition to having an in-depth knowledge of the British Singles Charts and The Guinness Book of Sporting Records, you should also be able to repeat all television lager, Cinzano and Campari commercials verbatim, and your data banks should contain copious scraps of information such as the following:

1) Names of Derby winners since the turn of the century
2) Kevin Keegan's favourite breakfast cereal
3) The combined birthweight of the England 1982 World Cup Squad.
4) Star signs of the famous
5) Barbara Windsor's bust measurement
6) The plots of Every Which Way But Loose, Dirty Harry, Freebie and The Bean, Smokey and The Bandit, Mad Max, Rollerball, Death Race 2000, and Friday The Thirteenth Part Three in 3D
7) The words to *Viva España*
8) Jocky Wilson's preferred brand of underarm deodorant
9) Fiona Richmond's telephone number.

With the help of your data banks, you should also be able to speak authoritatively on the following burning issues:

1) Was God an astronaut?
2) Are the Russians controlling our weather?
3) Prophesies of Nostradamus
4) Dolly Parton: the silicon implant question

The Wally look

Wally credibility means *dressing* like a Wally too.

Many people fondly imagine that all you have to do to achieve the Wally look is to bung on a mouldering T-shirt or acrylic pully in the morning, drag a razor over the bum fluff (slicing the top off a few spots in the process), splash on

Arthur Scargill 'Nylon-look' hair

Chunky cardigan

The Handsome Brut

Beer gut

Chunky gold signet rings

Man-eating Dobermann

Love bite

Exposed midriff revealing solarium sun tan.

The Harlow Harpie

Ghetto blaster

The Acrylic Kid

100% acrylic sweater

St Christopher medallion

Identity bracelet

Stay prest strides

C+A trainers

Mirror shades

Elastoplast to cover minor skin abrasions caused by repeated headbanging

Bum fluff

Brain bucket or skid lid

The Hell's Wally

Derry boots

27

half a gallon of Brut and thus to go around looking – and in the case of the Hell's Wally, smelling – pretty much like the proverbial pig's breakfast.

Of course, this is a myth.

The Wally Look has to be worked at. Even the dragged-through-a-hedge-backwards look favoured by the Hell's Wally (see p. 27) involves hours of preparation if you're going to Get It Right. It's not just a question of clothes – it's personal grooming too. There's the hair to attend to, the pimples and pustules to anoint with Calomine Lotion; and then comes the purely practical problem of how to insinuate your legs into those festering drainpipe jeans without causing them to disintegrate altogether. The jeans, that is. If you're going to go for the Handsome Brut look (see p. 26), it could take you even longer; sometimes it's months before you find a shampoo that gives your hair that unique Arthur Scargill nylon toupee texture.

Another point that needs to be borne in mind is that the Wally Look is only *partly* to do with the way you dress or the way you comb – or appear not to comb – your hair. Just as important is that indefinable something in the set of your features or your stance generally that marks you out as a Wally – as someone who might well at some point in the past have been bodily ejected from Tiffany's on a Friday night, caught fare-dodging on the Underground, or incarcerated by Spanish police for pouring soap powder into municipal fountains in Madrid during World Cup Final Week. That subtle whiff of the out-and-out Wally can't be faked, just as it can't be taught. You've either Got It or you haven't.

For the time being, though, let's concentrate on what you *can* achieve by selecting the right clothes. The following notes on Wally attire should help you.

Underpants. When it comes to underpants, the true Wally dresses according to a simple maxim: 'If you want to raise a laugh, drop your trousers.' In certain circumstances, the mere act of appearing in public dressed only in your underpants is enough to establish that you're a Wally. But to ram the message home, make sure that your underpants are made of nylon and are inscribed with one or more of these mottos:

● Sex Appeal – Please give generously
● I don't know what ideas *you've* got, lady, but these are staying on.
● Greetings from Loch Ness
● Home of the Jolly Pink Giant
● Prodwell Hydraulic Research Establishment
● Pink and Perky
● Do Not Crush
● Flasher
● Vasectomised

Also acceptable are: American-style boxer shorts, string underpants, bikini briefs, sequinned jockstraps, posing pouches, and any underpants decorated with polka dots, Union Jacks or carnival stripes.

Vests. String vests are quintessentially Wally, and so are T-shirts *worn* as vests. But in both cases they should be clearly visible; either undo the top buttons of your shirt or wear a shirt made out of a man-made fibre that lets the vest or T-shirt show through.

Thermal underwear. This is only Wally if worn during a heatwave.

Trousers. Flared trousers, golfing slacks, Stay-Prest strides or denim jeans with buttons instead of a zip are Wally. All should be worn slightly short in order to display your jazzy socks to full advantage.

Shirts and ties. Matching shirts and ties, Englebert Humperdinck frilly dress shirts, polyester shirts dotted with racing cars, horses or other emblems are all acceptable items of Wally wear. Stripey shirts with white collars are *de rigueur* for the executive Wally (see p. 112), but note that the collars should *not* be detachable. Leisure shirts for disco wear should have giant collars that stretch right across the shoulders.

T-shirts, Sweatshirts, etc. T-shirts form a vital part of the Wally wardrobe, but a T-shirt with the *wrong* design or message on it is a glaring gaffe that can spell social disaster. Unless you're going to proclaim your membership of CAMRA or your loyalty to certain approved rock bands, stick to sanctioned legends such as the following:

- Oh Lord, help me to keep my big mouth shut until I know what I'm talking about
- Too much sex makes you late for work
- I'm with stupid
- Sod Off
- I am a virgin (but this is a very old T-shirt)
- Ormskirk College of Food Technology Rag Week (*or similar*)

Pullovers. Guernsies and hand-knitted originals are *out*! You *might* risk a navy-blue lambswool V-neck with greyhound motif and get away with it in a poor light, but the only way to be really safe is to stick to those Wally classics, the diamond-patterned acrylic eyeball-searer or the heavy-knit white and brown belted cardigan or Wally Warmer.

Shoes. Shoes are the Cinderella of the Wally's wardrobe. Hush Puppies, C & A Trainers, possibly a heavyweight two-tone pair with multicoloured laces for best — it's not wise to sport anything too fancy when a major part of your daily routine consists of kicking Coke cans around shopping precincts, shinning up lamposts and leaping flights of stairs in multi-storey car parks.

Suits. Suits tend to be worn only by executive or business Wallies, or by Wallies attending weddings, funerals or making court appearances following night-club brawls. Should be a three-piece number in black, dark blue or beige enabling the wearer to pass as Vito Corleone's right-hand man.

Personal adornment. No CND or SDP lapel badges, please. Heavy gold signet rings, plastic key-rings in the form of biscuits, gold 'ingot' pendants with the hallmark on the front, identity bracelets, St Christopher medallions, tie clips, arm bracelets, mirror shades, imitation crocodile-skin belts with large buckles in the form of the wearer's initials, belts with purses attached or huge bunches of keys dangling from them: all are acceptable. Many people apparently fail to see the point of wearing an identity bracelet. In fact it has a simple practical purpose. It's for those grim mornings when you wake up with a splitting headache and can't remember who the hell you are.

Recognising your fellow-Wally

Wally credibility means being able to spot another Wally a mile off. The difficulty here is that everybody has their own idea of what a Wally is. You no doubt have yours. The person who cornered you in a train compartment and talked about custom cars all the way from Euston to Inverness was a Wally. The joker in your office who stuck the receiver to your phone with Superglue was a Wally. The bloke down the road who claims to know this bloke who knows this other bloke whose brother's in the S.A.S. is a Wally.

The point is: you think you know. Everybody thinks they know.

In actual fact, spotting a Wally isn't that simple any more.

Not all Wallies go around with woolly bobble hats pulled down over their eyes. There are plainclothes or 'closet' Wallies too: outwardly respectable people doing outwardly respectable jobs who've probably never worn an RAC

Lombard Rally or Avon Tyres anorak in their life; people you'd never suspect of being Wallies – until one day they strip down to their Union Jack underpants and insist on showing you their tattoos.

Then there are the soft-spoken retiring types who wouldn't so much as break wind in a telephone box – until they astonish you at the annual company dinner by leaping to their feet, seizing the nearest microphone, rattling off a stream of side-splitting mother-in-law jokes or celebrity impressions, performing tricks with their toupee and rounding off the act by setting fire to their chest hair with a cigarette lighter.

Even more disconcerting are the people who look like Wallies or are doing jobs traditionally performed by Wallies – sticking labels on tins of Cook-In Sauce at Tescos or selling electrical goods at Comet – who turn out not to be Wallies at all; instead they're History of Art students from Oxford working in their vac, Shirley Conran's offspring slumming it, or journalists gathering data for articles in *New Society*.

So how on earth do you tell? There's no easy answer to this one, but you may find it helpful to consult the guide on pp. 34-35.

The Wally Who's Who

In order to achieve Wally credibility you must know who's who in the Wally World.

So who are the big names? An abridged list of current members of the International Order of the Sick Parrot can be found in the Reference Section at the end of this book, (see p. 122). In the meantime it's also instructive to take a look at a few individuals who for one reason or another *fail* to be Wallies, and ask yourself where they're going wrong.

Why is it, for example, that Paul Gambaccini patently fails to be a Wally, while Peter Powell, Tony Blackburn, Jonathan King and Dave Lee Travis are not only past masters of the art but probably couldn't be anything else if they tried? Is it just to do with his occasional appearances on the arts programme Kaleidoscope, or is there some deeper reason?

Why is it that Sir John Betjeman repeatedly manages to miss being a Wally while his two fellow-wordsmiths Cyril Fletcher and Pam Ayres hit the mark unerringly every time? With all those years of practice behind him, you'd have thought he could have managed to Get It Right by now.

Clearly, many famous personalities in the sporting, entertainment or cultural world fail to be Wallies simply through lack of motivation. Bjorn Borg is a case in point. As a tennis player he was certainly a hard man to beat, but when it came to being a Wally, John McEnroe could wipe the floor with him every time.

A similar case, this time in the field of journalism, is Bernard Levin. The looks and the voice are both highly promising, but when you stop and listen to what the man is actually saying, you realise that he's not merely failing to be a Wally, he's actually going out of his way to avoid being one.

The Levins and the Borgs are hard enough to fathom, but even more exasperating are the ones who teeter on the brink of being Wallies but seem to lack the courage and dedication to go the whole way. The Terry Wogans of this world, for instance, who after years of providing a moderately Wally form of early-morning entertainment and hosting the agreeably Wally Blankety Blank, suddenly go and throw away all chance of being a culture-hero by coming on strong as a compere to an upmarket TV chat show. The Henry Kelly types who one minute are scaling the peaks of Wally achievement on Game For A Laugh and then, next thing you know, are making ill-advised bids for intellectual respectability on the BBC Midweek programme.

The fundamental mistake these people make is to believe that you can somehow try and come over as being thoughtful, rational and articulate and yet retain your credibility as a Wally. It just can't be done.

If you want to appear on, say, Question Time, and still be a Wally, the only way to do it is to abandon all pretence of being thoughtful, rational and articulate and be silly instead.

Not normally Wallies	Frequently Wallies
Eastern mystics*	Post Office clerks
Brain surgeons	Wimbledon line-judges
International tax lawyers	Accordionists
Concert pianists**	Hi-fi buffs
Chess Grand Masters	Tolkein fans
Mastermind champions***	Traffic wardens
International hit men	Radio 1 disc jockeys
Marriage Guidance Counsellors	Former Metropolitan Police Commissioners
Forensic scientists	Train spotters
Financial Times leader writers	Griddle chefs
Polyglots	Darts commentators
Sanskrit scholars	Morris dancers
	Rank Xerox reps
	Figure-skaters
	Rotarians
	Members of the United Nations Security Council
	Buskers
	Fairground barkers
	Cocktail waiters
	Scaffolding contractors
	Town planners
	Taxidermists
	Radio hams
	Railway modellers

Notes
*Eastern mystics. It is possible to be an Eastern Mystic and a Wally *if* you wear a nylon quilted anorak over your robes and distribute leaflets in Oxford Street.

**Concert pianists. Can be Wallies *if* they wear red tuxedos, look pretty, stick to the slow and easy stuff and sign lucrative recording contracts with K-Tel.

Always complete and utter Wallies

Swimming-pool attendants
Motorcycle stunt riders
Demolition derby drivers
Handbell teams
Square-dancing enthusiasts
Jehovah's Witnesses
Headline-writers for the *Sun*
Game-show hosts
Local radio disc jockeys
Druids
Bikers
Nude hang-gliders
Pole-sitters
Roadies
Yodellers
Gurners
Gnomologists
Members of the Sealed Knot
Scientologists/Mormons
Superannuated hippies
Monocyclists
'It's A Knock-Out' teams
Berkshire Tuttimen

Wurzels
Welly-chuckers
Stumblebums
Bicycle jousters
Bollard leapers
Bellyfloppers
The Miss World jury
Flat Earthers
Canary fanciers
Champion pickled egg eaters
Fork-benders
All-in wrestlers
Male models
Members of the Official
    Raving Monster Loony Party
Loblolly men
Blow Football enthusiasts
Photo-booth nobblers
Bottom pinchers
Balloon dancers
Ticket touts
Beermat collectors

***Obviously, you can be a Mastermind Champion and a Wally if you go on to join the regulars on the BBC Start The Week team.

Further observations
Any Questions hecklers are not necessarily Wallies.

The Maori who exposed his buttocks to the Royal Family but chose the one moment when they were looking the other way was unlucky. He tried to be a Wally and failed.

But since the other panellists are very often being silly too, there's a grave danger that your gesture might pass unnoticed and that you might find yourself being lumped together with the Michael Heseltines, the Willie Whitelaws and the Eric Heffers – people who are not in fact Complete Wallies, just pretty good imitations.

Perhaps all in all it's safest to follow the example of Tony Blackburn, Peter Powell and most successful Wally notables, and resist the temptation to pronounce sagely on world affairs. If you're a true Wally celebrity you should in any case be far too busy opening supermarkets.

HOW TO BE A WALLY ON WHEELS

At first sight, this looks like a pretty daunting topic. Basically, however, it breaks down into two major areas:

1) How to choose a Wally car and equip it with Wally accessories
2) How to drive it like a Wally

The first point all too often gets overlooked by novice Wallies, but it's every bit as important as the second. Lane-hopping or straddling the white line in a less-than-Wally car such as a Fiat Panda is fine as far as it goes. But the danger here is that you could create – as well as exasperation, which of course is the object of the exercise – *confusion* in the minds of other roadusers. They might think, for example, that you've simply had a hard day at the office or that you're on your way back from a Private View or a wine-tasting and that you're being a Wally more or less by accident.

The only way to remove the confusion is both to drive like a Wally and make sure that the car you drive shouts *Wally* loud and clear to every other motorist. This section is intended to help you do both.

But first, a word or two about the mental attitude you will need to adopt towards your car.

If you're a Wally, the very word 'wheels' should be enough to bring you out in goose bumps. It should conjure up a whole world of magically enticing leisure activities brought suddenly within your reach: fascinating one-way systems and intricate spaghetti junctions to explore; famous accident black spots to visit; historic cathedral cities to bypass; and at last that trip up to Coventry to try your hand at ten-pin bowling or see the Barron Knights in cabaret becomes a real possibility!

In the driving seat of your dream on wheels you are no longer just Barry Whatsisname from Accounts who's just been passed over for promotion for the sixth time in as many years – you're a king, a demon, a force to be reckoned with, and your souped-up Capri leaves the boss's boring old Rover standing at the lights every time. Your sex-life looks up, too, when you've got wheels. If you turn up for a date with the average female Wally on nothing more macho than a bicycle, the chances are that you won't get very far. But if you screech to a halt outside her house in a gleaming Escort plastered with Go Faster stripes and dripping with accessories, you'll probably be halfway to putting another notch on your belt before you even get to the front door, and a couple of Snowballs, a Carpenters tape playing softly on the car stereo and a few sotto voce sweet nothings in the car park of the Moon and Parrot will do the rest.

As well as the huge range of exciting things you can do with your motor, there's also the tremendous kick you get simply out of owning it. There's that matchless pride you feel as you run your hand lovingly over the bodywork, playfully fondle the fluffy dice or miniature football boots hanging from the rear-view mirror, or offer the little doggie in the back window his morning bowl of Winalot. Learn to treasure these moments of quiet intimacy between owner and vehicle. They are what being a Wally on wheels is all about.

Which motor?

Learning the complex skills involved in being a Wally driver will always take time and nearly always involve at some point careering off the road and ending up upside down in a field of Brussels sprouts. Choosing a Wally car is a relatively simple matter of paying over the odds for the right credibility-boosting model, and should be painless enough if you follow a few basic guidelines.

First, Wallies *don't* drive Renaults, Citroens, Fiats, Ford Fiestas, Volkswagen Polos, Land Rovers or Range Rovers – or rather, they *can*, but these are not intrinsically Wally marques. Wallies tend to steer clear of foreign makes in general, on the grounds that you can't get the parts. You can of course order the parts from a garage and have them fitted professionally, but it's an important Wally credo that spares hunted down in scrapyards and fitted yourself in your spare time make your car go faster.

The true Wally also scorns the notion of choosing a car on the basis of ease of parking, size of boot, or fuel economy; he sees gas-guzzling, like Black Label-guzzling, as a token of virility. You have probably often heard one Wally say admiringly of another; 'He can't half put it away.' The same principle applies to cars.

So what kind of cars does the discerning Wally go for? It varies according to need. Speed-freak Wallies opt for sporty models that belch out clouds of choking exhaust fumes as they're hammered up to seventy in the Bus Lane, putting the fear of God into other road-users. Wimpier Wallies in trilbies and car coats will probably prefer something more homely – an Morris Marina perhaps: the perfect vehicle in which to chug along and admire the scenery at the head of a three-mile tail-back. Many hard-core auto-enthusiast Wallies plump for cars which never actually move at all, but spend their entire life on bricks in the front garden, while the owner grovels around underneath with a monkey-wrench and a spanner, the object of much ignorant derision from girl-friends, neighbours and passersby.

In general, when buying a car, you should look for the following essential features:

1) An engine with 'poke'
2) Leg-room in the front
3) Leg-over room in the back
4) An ample glove compartment. This makes an excellent home for Man-Size Kleenex Tissues, condoms, Airwicks, back numbers of *Custom Car* and *Auto-Car*, and once a year the envelope containing the £10 note that will see your motor safely through its M.O.T.
5) A large rear window ledge to accomodate fluffy dice, nodding dogs with eyes that light up when you brake, dangling trolls and luminous green spiders, crochet cushions and stereo speakers.
6) A cracked silencer
7) Vast wheel arches, so that you can fit 18-inch

aluminium sports wheels at the back and give your motor that sloping-down-at-the-front look. Also useful for concealing smuggled bottles of Creme de Menthe on your way back from your Continental holiday.

Accessories

To a certain extent, even the non-Wally cars already mentioned could be made to pass as Wally if you equipped them with the right accessories. But only up to a point. A Morris Traveller is never going to look particularly Wally, even if you fur-line the interior and train plastic roses up the timbering.

On a Ford Capri or Cortina, however, you can wreak a really stunning transformation by fitting the following refinements:

1) Autoplas whaletail or quatrofoil boot spoiler
2) Fog lamps with chequered covers
3) Supernumerary brake lights
4) Go Faster stripes
5) Leather or leopard-skin steering wheel glove
6) Musical car horn. Ideally Colonel Bogey, but La Cucaracha, Oh Susannah, Strangers in the Night and the theme tune from The Dukes Of Hazzard will do.
7) Nudge and Roll bars
8) Giant exhaust in gleaming chrome, preferably of the 'bolt-on' variety, *i.e.* serving no practical purpose whatsoever
9) San Francisco number plate
10) Green tinted sunstripe for the windscreen, with your name and your girl-friend's stencilled on it (*unless* you're called Rupert, James, Charles, Sebastian or Julian)

Wally window stickers

The following rear window stickers are valuable Wally credibility-boosters and can safely be fixed to all Wally cars:

- My other car's a Porsche
- This car is a recycled Ferrari
- When God made women drivers he was only joking
- Jim could not fix this
- Happiness is driving over a Traffic Warden's foot
- Passion Wagon – Don't laugh, your daughter may be inside
- 0-60 in 30 minutes
- Don't honk. I'm going as fast as I can, dammit!
- Please pass quietly – driver asleep
- Speed on, brother – Hell ain't half full yet
- This car wants to be a Rolls Royce when it grows up
- Windsurfers do it standing up
- Glider pilots stay up longer
- Rugger players have leather balls
- Only screwing beats canoeing
- Preserve wild life. Pickle a Traffic Warden
- Save energy – Make love slowly

Window stickers that don't belong in Wally cars

1) Any sticker bearing the National Trust oakleaves emblem – an obvious no-no.

2) Green 'Nothing to Declare' stickers. These are used by Volvo drivers as a subtle way of insinuating that they can not only afford an expensive car but an expensive Continental holiday as well. There's therefore not much point in sticking one on a rusting old Ford Zephyr that you picked up for a song via the back pages of your local freesheet.

3) *Caution – show dogs in transit.* Not a Wally sticker unless the dogs in question are Mexican Hairless or Chihuahuas which you're entering for the novelty class.

4) *Carry a kidney donor card.* Borderline. To carry a kidney donor card is exactly the kind of public-spirited act that most Wallies would instinctively avoid. On the other hand, what the sticker also says is '*I* carry a kidney donor card' – and if you think that's going to deter anybody from driving into the back of you, or that anyone is really remotely interested in what you propose to do with your kidneys, you're a Wally.

Guidebooks that don't belong in Wally cars

One kind of book which you will definitely *not* be needing is the expensively produced tome that purports to tell you where to eat 'just off the motorway'. To the true Wally, the willingness of otherwise rational human beings to turn off a motorway and drive for miles down winding pot-holed minor roads, spattering their motor with mud and cow-dung and scratching the paintwork on brambles in search of some dive full of rural geriatrics, is one of the great mysteries of modern times. Many of these so-called pubs do not even serve Black Label and offer nothing more exciting in the way of pub entertainment than a skittle alley out the back and a dartboard with half the stuffing coming out of it. In many of them, too, you can't even stand up straight without knocking your head on some hulking great fourteenth century beam riddled with deathwatch beetle. When a Wally has to pause for refreshment in mid-journey, he eats, drinks and disports himself at the motorway services – or, if he's travelling on a major road, he simply whips out the picnic kit and tucks in by the roadside. You should learn to do the same (see p. 66).

Books with titles such as *The AA/Reader's Digest Treasury of the English Countryside* or *The Hidden Places of Britain* also get a resounding Bronx cheer from Wallies and should not be seen on the back seat of your motor. To a Wally, 'Country' means either John Denver and Dolly Parton, or the dull bits between the towns that aren't lit up at night. He likes urban sprawl, and he's found one or two interesting things to do in Beauty Spots, but in the country he's like a fish out of water. He also finds the silence unnerving.

THE WALLY HIGHWAY CODE

You've now chosen your car. You've paid for it – either with a suitcase full of used notes or by means of a generous loan from Mercantile Credit which you will spend the rest of your natural life trying to repay. You've equipped it with all the accessories – the stickers, the stripes, the dice and so on. Now the time has come for you to venture out on the roads and learn how to be a Sunday driver, not just on Sunday, but *every* day of the week.

This takes practice. Don't be too disappointed if at first you find you can drive to work and back without once mounting the kerb or ploughing into a line of yellow plastic No Parking cones. Stick at it. Eventually you'll find, as thousands of other Wally motorists have found before you, that the ever-present risk of winding up on a Driving Without Due Care and Attention rap, or finding yourself in a mangled heap in the middle of a roundabout on the North Circular, adds that vital extra dimension of motoring enjoyment.

Lane indiscipline. The diagram shows how to achieve very satisfying results by the simple expedient of being in the wrong lane. You're in a left-hand filter lane; the motorists behind naturally assume you're going to *turn* left – yet mysteriously, when the green arrow lights up, you remain stationary. You've had a last-minute change of plan and have decided to go straight on instead. Result: a deafening barrage of honking, effing and blinding from the cars behind.

When the main lights change and the traffic in the right-hand lane begins to move forward, you have two options open to you. You can either (a): suddenly, and without giving any advance warning, veer round to the head of the right-hand queue as if you were overtaking on the inside; or (b): further exasperate the drivers in the left-hand lane by just sitting there like a lemon with your indicator going, waiting until some charitably disposed driver in the right-hand lane decides to stop and let you pull over.

The mini-roundabout. The diagram shows three Wallies at a mini-roundabout. Each is completely baffled by the right-of-way system and is therefore waiting nervously for one of the others to make the first move. What happens next – if anything at all – is anybody's guess. All three could simultaneously make a sudden dash for it and collide in the middle; alternatively, they could stay put for the rest of the afternoon, while huge queues of traffic form behind them in all three directions and the entire traffic system in the surrounding area slowly grinds to a total standstill – in which case, there's the additional benefit that Wallies stranded in the resulting jams will be able to get out of their cars, stretch their legs and brew-up by the roadside. (The adjoining diagram is also available as a novelty drinkmat, entitled 'Still Life').

Overtaking. The only important rule to observe here is that wherever you overtake – on a blind corner, the brow of a hill, or a level crossing – you should afterwards immediately reduce speed until you're going slower than the car you've just overtaken. This is a particularly effective tactic on a narrow or winding road where the other driver has no opportunity to overtake you back.

Driving through gaps. An essential skill for the Wally driver is being able to *mis*judge the width of his own car. The two diagrams illustrate in a simplified form how this skill should be applied. Wally A has braked sharply and slowed down to a crawl in order to drive through a gap that would actually take a juggernaut, giving the driver behind such a nasty shock that he's swallowed his dentures and gone careering off the road.

Wally B has gone to the opposite extreme. He has driven at breakneck speed through a gap that he *correctly* judged

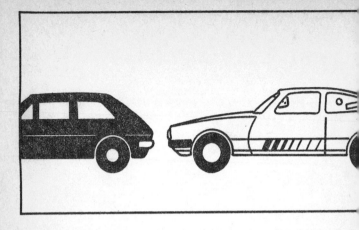

to be just that crucial couple of inches too small for his car, ripping the wing mirrors off the stationary vehicles parked on either side, doing appreciable damage to their paintwork and scattering panic-stricken cyclists and pedestrians in all directions.

Either of these two approaches is permissible.

Parking symmetrically. If you're looking for a parking spot in a busy town centre and you're lucky enough to find a spot big enough for *two* cars, try and remember to park exactly in the middle and to leave half a car's length at each end. Leaving a great big gap at one end is asymmetrical and looks messy.

The Pelican crossing. There is always confusion surrounding the exact significance of the flashing orange light on a Pelican crossing. In fact, it's all very simple. The flashing light tells you, the motorist, that if there *are* any pedestrians foolhardy enough to be using the crossing at the time, you are perfectly entitled to run them over. If, on the other hand, there are no pedestrians in sight, *you must stop*. There are, naturally, borderline situations in which you may have to make a difficult choice between putting the wind up pedestrians and annoying the hell out of the driver behind, but in nine cases out of ten it's obvious which course of action is going to get the best results.

Come blow your Colonel Bogey car horn. If you use it to its full potential, your Colonel Bogey car horn can be an instrument of enormous expressive power, capable of conveying a host of different messages. You are *not* getting the most out of it if you simply use it to warn people that you'll drive into the back of them if they don't get out of your way. Other messages include:

Hello Gorgeous
Oi! Don't I know you from somewhere?
I couldn't give a monkey's if this *is* a built-up neighbourhood
Naff off
Last one to the Watford Gap's a Turkey
Just testing.

What to do after a road accident. Look seriously into the whole question of car insurance.

Taking a pride in your motor

One of the great joys of being a Wally on wheels is being able to pile into the motor on a Saturday or Sunday afternoon, zoom off to an area of outstanding natural beauty, pull in at an officially designated picnic site and give those brimming car ashtrays a really thorough clear out. In fact, while you're at it, it's worth giving the whole of the inside of your motor a good going over. You'll be surprised at some of the things you find wedged under the arm rests or under the back seat: fag ends, banana skins and orange peel, half-eaten chips, girlie mags, Kentucky Fried Chicken boxes, crushed Seven-Up cans – it's just amazing how quickly litter accumulates, and if you don't have a purge every couple of weeks or so, you can find yourself driving around in the company of a great reeking pile of waste-paper, cigarette ash and rotting fruit and vegetable matter which can not only pose a serious threat to health but can also impede leg-overs and obstruct your view through the rear windscreen. It doesn't make any kind of sense to let your car get into that kind of state, so do yourself a favour: get rid of the stuff before you catch some horrible disease off it – and if you can find a pleasant spot with a bit of a view in which to go about this frankly rather unpleasant task, and perhaps even have a bit of fun as you scatter it around the countryside, so much the better.

While we're on the subject of beautiful surroundings, it's also worth remembering that no matter how carefully you look after your motor, no matter how much love you give it under the bonnet, there's always a risk that one day it'll develop some terminal mechanical fault and become no longer economic to run. When that day comes, don't prolong the agony unnecessarily: drive or tow it out to a stretch of National Trust parkland, remove the wheels, the fluffy dice, the leopardskin steering wheel glove and anything else that's either still serviceable or that you simply can't bear to part with, and give the poor old banger as dignified a burial as possible, in a stream, pond or clump of trees. It's surely worth risking a paltry fine to know that the motor that gave you so many hours of pleasure is now part of Nature's ever-changing canvas.

One final word of advice. If you're lucky enough to find a ravine to dump it in – don't forget to jump out first.

Before concluding this guide to how to be a Wally on wheels, a brief look at two closely related topics: mopeds and motorbikes; and CB radio.

Mopeds and motorbikes. No very clear guidelines can be laid down here as to what makes are most desirable. *Any* motorbike, moped or even pushbike *can* be Wally if you make it rear up like a Liberty horse and ride it on the back wheel only. However, simply falling off isn't good enough. Anybody can do that.

Don't underestimate these more modest forms of transport. It's surprising how much impact you can make on a quiet suburban cul-de-sac even with a puny Honda 50 if you repeatedly ride it up and down in the small hours of the morning, practising your gear changes. In fact, even if you remain completely stationary and just rev it up in your front garden you can very soon find yourself being voted Public Enemy Number One.

In order to be a real Wally on a motorbike, don't feel you have to go for the 500cc models. 75ccs are ample – better in fact, because the lower the engine capacity, the better the noise-to-performance ratio. The moped is hard to beat in this respect. Even at absurdly low speeds it makes a noise like a bee in a biscuit tin, and the volume increases disproportionately as the needle crawls agonisingly up to the thirty mark. Also, being a Wally on a motorbike is less to do with *what* you ride than the way you ride it. If you think that 75cc of raw power between your legs is going to make you the Barry Sheene of Upper Norwood, you'll be a Wally and no mistake.

CB Radio. CB radio is more than just an accessory in your car – it's an essential. This is not only because it gives you an excuse to stick an enormous aerial on your boot (you ought to have one of those already), but because upwards of 350,000 other Wallies up and down the country are already enthusiastic CB users, and you don't want to get left out. The advantages of CB are obvious. As a Wally Breaker you can:

1) Direct visiting CB-ers to interesting local bottlenecks and recommend greasy spoon roadside diners.

2) Be propositioned by gay long-distance lorry drivers. (If he enquires about the size of your 'rig' or 'thunderstick' suspect the worst.)

3) Receive the very latest up-to-the-minute information on road accidents on your patch. This will enable you to be first on the scene, whip out the emergency warning triangle which up till now has been languishing unused in the back of your car, generally make a bloody nuisance of yourself as police, ambulance and fire-brigade clear away the wreckage and stand around looking officious and public-spirited and congratulating yourself on having played a major role in the rescue effort.

Choice of 'handle'. The first requirement of the Wally CB-er is to adopt a suitable pseudonym or 'handle'. Given the type of handles used by CB-ers — Kinky Knickers, Speedy Lady, Green Gremlin, Twinkle Toes, Bush Baby and so on — it should be obvious that your main problem here is going to be thinking up a daft name that hasn't already been thought of by thousands of other Wallies. If you're really stumped, try one of the following:

Big Girl's Blouse
Simple Simon
Gumboil
Cheeky Chappie
Silly Billy
Butterball
Pimple Bonce
Cloth Ears

Sick Parrot

What the hell do you talk about? Transcripts of conversations between CB-ers reveal that if you're really prepared to work at it, it is possible to drip on literally for hours without once saying anything noteworthy or remarkable. But don't expect to be able to master this skill straight away. For the time being, it'll probably be as much as you can do to select the right frequency without driving into the back of a milk float.

There are two possible approaches to the art of conversing on CB Radio, one very much preferable to the other. The safest way is to stick to topics on which it's virtually impossible to say anything interesting. The other less satisfactory method is to choose potentially interesting topics but to be grindingly dull about them, which tends to require thought. Worse, there's also a risk that you may accidentally let slip some fascinating or blindingly brilliant *aperçu* and suddenly find that your listener has retuned in disgust, leaving you talking into thin air. Topics to avoid include the following:

The active part you take in National Trust fund-raising
Ballet
Batik
Natural Childbirth

THE WALLY AT LARGE

How to be a Wally Consumer

In the eyes of many people, being a Wally shopper is child's play. It's like shoplifting in reverse. All you do is whizz round with your supermarket trolley snatching cheap and nasty items off the shelves more or less at random – things you don't really need at all. Unlike the shoplifter, however, you pay for them on your way out.

Needless to say, there's a great deal more to it than that.

Being a Wally shopper means striking a very careful balance between paying *less* than you ought for essentials such as food, clothing, bedding and furniture and so on – and *more* than you ought for the luxuries: Sodastreams, solenoid-operated cat flaps, electronic door chimes that play Stars and Stripes, and remote-control tellies.

In practice it's not always easy to distinguish between these two categories. A 20 per cent reduction in the price of candlewick loo seat covers at John Lewis can very often persuade you that these are not luxury items at all but essential adornments to your home – which indeed they are if you're a Wally. However, since they're probably still absurdly overpriced for what they are, you're safe to go ahead and buy. Much the same applies to 'bargain' quadrophonic systems, rowing machines, plastic cocktail cabinets in the form of antique globes on castors, and reproduction four-poster beds. Buying *any* of these is bound to up your credibility as a Wally, since whatever the price, it's always going to be too much.

In general, when out shopping, try and observe the following simple rules.

Shop where you see the sign 'Prices Slashed'. This doesn't mean that you should sit down in advance and ask yourself 'What do I need?' and then go out and shop around until you find somewhere that's selling it for a reasonable price – that's exactly the mistake many normal shoppers make. The point is that you should head straight for the signs saying 'Unbeatable bargains' or (surely the five most beautiful words in the English language) 'Buy One, Get One Free', inspect whatever's on offer and somehow convince yourself that you can find a use for it. In nine cases out of ten you'll end up with a product that's still overpriced and that you didn't want or need in the first place.

Look for the free gift. Ideally the freebie should be every bit as desirable as the item actually purchased. *E.g.* a free sherry glass, an E.T. doll or pliable Smurf that melts when you leave it on the radiator, a voucher or coupon which when combined with a ridiculously large number of packet tops or other proofs of purchase, entitles you to a free haircut, a pocket calculator, 30p off the price of a prawn cocktail at a Schooner Inn, a free day's parking in the car park of the Ladbroke Dragonara Hotel, Leeds, or a chance to enter a competition in which you stand a very slim chance indeed of winning two weeks in a cottage overlooking a firing range on Salisbury Plain.*

Look for the hidden defect. Ask yourself: does the product you are about to buy contain a hidden snag that will only become apparent after you've taken it home and thrown away the bag and label? In the case of a garment, this could be a tendency to fall to pieces when exposed to strong sunlight, or to bring on attacks of asthma or hay fever or radiation sickness, or for the colour to drain out in the wash, staining your novelty underpants and 'I choked Linda Lovelace' T-shirt a splendidly eye-catching dayglo orange. If the answer's yes, buy it.

Resist high-pressure sales talk. Shop assistants, particularly in the hi-fi and men's outfitting line, can be very

---

* However, to bulk-buy a certain brand of washing powder because you get free British Rail travel vouchers with it is not necessarily the act of a Wally. Only if you haven't got a washing machine.

persuasive, and in their frantic eagerness to sell you a product that is very often genuinely worthless and exorbitantly priced, they can sometimes give you the entirely erroneous impression that it may have something going for it after all. In your disappointment at finding that it's not the complete waste of money you were banking on, you will then lose interest, walk out of the shop — and kick yourself later when you realise you missed a once-in-a-lifetime opportunity to pay good money for a first-class load of old rubbish.

Shops No Wally Should be Seen Dead In

Antiquarian Booksellers. Wally reading matter is bought at newsagents and tobacconists along with Mars Bars, fags and plastic combs. If you want a book with that well-thumbed look, the place to go is the bargain racks at Susan Reynolds.

Health Food Shops. As a Wally you should be able to break wind wherever and whenever the occasion demands without the help of red kidney beans, lentils, brown rice or other aids to flatulence.

Interflora. Wallies don't say it with flowers — at least, not real ones. If you want to show her you care, send her a bad taste greetings card from John Menzies or, for special occasions, a Wallygram. This where three Wallies in football scarves turn up on her doorstep and spray her with beer from a Party Four.

The Waitrose on the King's Road. Shopping in a supermarket that sells fresh Fennel, Ochra and Calabrise can seriously damage your Wally credibility.

Christian Bookshops. For you, inspirational literature means *101 Uses of a Dead Cat*.

Buying through classified ads. One of the secrets of being a Wally shopper lies in avoiding simply buying second-rate or shoddy goods and in knowing where you can lay your hands on goods that are shoddy, second-rate and Wally too. This is where the Under a Fiver column of your local newspaper or freesheet can come in handy. A typical week's offerings usually include: Draylon seat covers in a variety of exciting shades; multi-coloured ex-Bed and Breakfast nylon sheets to snag your toenails on; clapped-out Music Centres; china carthorses; Bri-nylon housecoats; assorted carpet squares – all on offer at a give-away £4.99.

Items of bed linen or clothing purchased through an Under a Fiver column should be approached with extreme caution, preferably while wearing full protective clothing and should on no account be handled until they have been left to soak for several days in a bath containing a powerful industrial cleansing agent. This should remove stubborn stains and all but the very hardiest forms of insect or fungal life.

Shopping by mail. Shopping by mail involves an element of risk which should appeal to your sporting instincts. You never know quite what you're going to end up with. You could order a gilt carriage clock and be sent a cartwheel spice rack; you could order a Wellington boot tidy and end up with a hostess trolley. Alternatively, the mail order company to whom you've just sent a substantial cheque could suddenly cease trading and mysteriously vanish off the face of the earth. The next thing you know, there they are, featured in an hilarious item on That's Life.

How to buy a sumptuous hand-crafted Objet D'art which you will be proud to display in your home and cherish for all time. One of the most obvious ways to show that you're a Wally consumer is to send off for one of the numerous commemorative collectors' items advertised in colour supplements and glossy magazines.

On the face of it, nothing could be more straightforward. You just fill in the tear-off order form, enclose a cheque for a colossal sum of money, stick it in the post, and hey presto, within twenty-eight days, along comes your immaculately tooled African Wild Life lamp-base – a miracle of craftsmanship and life-like detail which will survive to grace your home long after the various endangered species represented on it have disappeared off the face of the earth, turned into fur coats, hearth rugs, waste-paper baskets and ivory figurines for other Wallies to squander their money on.

Of course, buying a timeless artefact isn't quite as easy as all that. Stop and think about it for a moment. If it *was* that easy, everybody would be doing it. And if everybody was sending off for Royal Wedding Teaspoon Sets, they wouldn't be collectors' items any more.

The catch is this. In order to reach the cheque-book-at-the-ready stage, you must sincerely believe that the artefact that you are about to buy has been hand-made in the traditional way by Europe's finest master-craftsmen, using techniques handed down over the centuries – and *not* mass-produced in Stoke on Trent or turned out by sweated labour somewhere in the Third World.

In practice it takes a special breed of Wally to pull off such an astonishing feat of credulity.

So how do you, a novice, bridge the gullibility gap?

One relatively painless method is to read through the sample order form on p. 60 and practise signing your name at the bottom until you feel credulous enough to tackle the real thing.

ORDER FORM FOR SUMPTUOUS HAND-CRAFTED OBJET D'ART

Please enter with all possible speed my order for this superb

☐ Onyx table lighter
☐ Porcelain figure of Italian boy in straw hat
☐ Two-handed Anglo-Saxon cider quaffer
☐ 18th century oxo-cube dispenser
☐ Set of ornamental brass dildos
☐ Queen Anne fondue set

which has been produced to commemorate

☐ The War of Jenkyns' Ear
☐ The Raising of the *Mary Rose*
☐ The sinking of the *Belgrano*
☐ The 500th Glorious Year of *The Mousetrap*
☐ The Relief of Mafeking
☐ The International Year of the Wally

and contains a tastefully inset

☐ Pre-decimal threepenny bit
☐ Fragment of the True Cross
☐ Piece chipped off Stonehenge

I understand that this/these sublime artefact(s) has/have been

☐ Hand-painted by trained chimpanzees on the finest bone china,
☐ Richly bordered with 22 carat gold which will in no circumstances come off in my dish-washer,

and I look forward to receiving with it/them a Certificate of Authenticity attesting to its/their unique qualities and pointing out that if for any reason I am not satisfied with it/them, it is now too late to get my money back. I need not sent a cheque now. I understand that I will be invoiced immediately prior to the despatch of my SUMPTUOUS HAND-CRAFTED OBJET, by which time the price will have doubled. I also solemnly undertake not to complain and make a fuss when I discover that my SUMPTUOUS HAND-CRAFTED OBJET is only half the size of the one shown in the advert.

Name ..*A. Wally*..............................

Camping out for the January Sales

Camping out for the January Sales is a traditional Wally activity and an essential feature of the post-Christmas scene. But it can be dangerous and shouldn't be attempted by anyone who isn't in absolutely peak physical condition. At that time of year, those Oxford Street pavements can be mighty chilly, especially at night. Also, there are all kinds of problems involved in camping in a built-up area, particularly when you're liable to discover that all the nearest loos and telephone boxes are out of action because you vandalised them on your last trip up to the West End.

When queueing for the Sales, you will need:

1) Grappling irons
2) Pile ointment
3) Water divining rod
4) Shotgun, primed and loaded, to keep by your side at all times
5) A silly hat or enormous stripey scarf or giant teddy bear
6) Hunting knife strapped to your leg for close combat
7) Also, nowadays more and more people are giving sale-queueing a bad name by taking advantage of media publicity to promote deserving causes, or getting other people to sponsor them for every day they spend in the queue and donating the proceeds to charity. In order to dissociate yourself from these kind of antics, it's a good idea to take along a large placard making clear that you're in it purely for personal gain

Nobody said that being a Wally is all fun. Spending up to a week in a sleeping bag outside a department store certainly isn't. Nor is it like any camping holiday you've ever experienced. For a start, instead of being woken by the sound of cattle lowing in the adjoining meadow or Frenchmen clearing their nasal passages in the campsite washrooms, you're more likely to find yourself being kicked or prodded awake by muggers and vagrants demanding money with menaces, accidentally trampled by Hare

The Wally Imaginary Guitar Tutor

Yes, being a guitar hero is easy thanks to this step-by-step guide. *And you don't have to play a note!*

- No more poring over chord charts!
- No more painful callouses on the ends of your fingers!
- Astound your friends at Status Quo concerts!

Just stick a heavy metal album on the turntable of your Music Centre, turn the volume up full blast, and strain, strut, groan and grimace your way through these exciting poses and lurid facial contortions.

1 The Opening Stance

3 The Squealing Guitar Solo

2 The Real Heavy Number

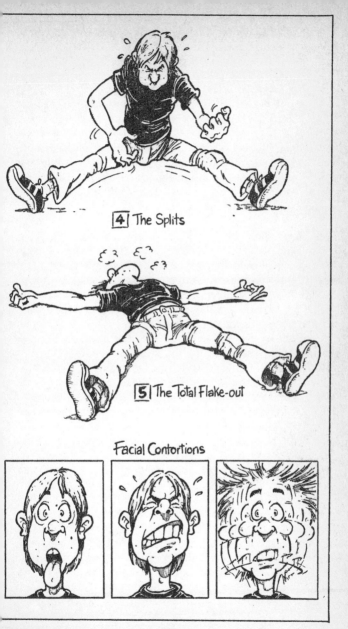

4 The Splits

5 The Total Flake-out

Facial Contortions

63

Krishna monks assembling for the first chant of the day, or greeted by a dawn chorus of jeers, catcalls and hoots of derision from dustmen, taxi-drivers and office cleaners on the early shift. Of course, it's all part of the experience – but it can be alarming if you're not expecting it.

Apart from all the more obvious unpleasantnesses, you should also be aware of two other potential hazards.

Nobbling. If you join a sale queue expecting cosy sing-songs round the campfire and a comradely 'We're all in this together' spirit, you're in for a nasty shock. All that stuff is strictly for the TV cameras. The truth is that even in daylight hours the atmosphere of simmering rivalry in a sale queue is something frightening; after the sun goes down and the shadows begin to lengthen, it's downright terrifying. When the doors are thrown open and those bargain-hungry punters stampede through into the store it's going to be every man for himself – and everybody in the queue knows it. The queue member who lets you borrow his copy of *Dalton's Weekly* one day could slit your throat for a place at the glassware counter the next.

So when you wake up in the mornings and you've managed to rub some of the circulation back into your aching limbs, *don't* go trying to curry favour by passing round your thermos and Benzedrine tablets; just be grateful that nobody from further down the queue has come round in the middle of the night and tried to remove your arms and legs with a machete.

Queue fatigue. After a few days' queueing, even the most fastidious type is going to look pretty much of a wreck: hair greasy and lifeless and impregnated with soot and exhaust fumes, eyes red through lack of sleep, three days' growth of beard … Some of the men will look fairly unprepossessing too. Be prepared for this, and *don't* go with unrealistic hopes of perhaps striking up some kind of relationship with a female queue-member. Most of the women you meet in sale queues probably won't be your type anyway – they're usually the kind that can turn the bathtaps on and off just by scowling at them.

The joy of supermarket trolley cruising

Jumping over rows of double-decker buses on a motorbike or leaping out of hot-air balloons and dangling by your ankles from lengths of knicker elastic can be fun, but unfortunately they both involve a bit of advance planning – and that means they're beyond the scope of all but a few very dedicated Wallies.

Cruising around in a supermarket trolley, though, is something *all* Wallies can and should have a go at. It doesn't involve any prior organisation, it's just as enjoyable – and it's free.

This is not to say that it's entirely without risk. Goodness knows, it's hard enough pushing a trolley around Tesco's when all it's got in it is a pair of Bachelor's Cup-A-Soups, a pre-cooked Lasagne for two and a packet of chicken drumsticks. It's *doubly* hard when you're wrestling to control a runaway trolley containing two or perhaps even three Wallies, all of them singing at the tops of their voices, waving football scarves and scattering empty crisp packets and Dr Pepper cans in all directions.

Unless you're dead set on winding up in the casualty department, it pays to follow a few simple precepts.

1) If you're going to be a passenger, remember to remove the shopping first. Sitting perched for any length of time on top of a frozen turkey can adversely affect your sex-life – quite apart from which, it's very annoying to discover later when unpacking your purchases that you've got a dozen broken eggs and two packets of crushed Waffles on your hands.

2) Try to resist the temptation to trolley-cruise down the ramps of multi-storey carparks. These are reserved for Wallies in cars pretending to be Starsky and Hutch, and the speeds they get up to on those blind corners can be quite frightening.

3) Up to a point, the unpredictability of a supermarket trolley is what gives it its charm. But for God's sake, if you're the one who's pushing, and you're on a slope, *don't let go*. Those little castors on the front have got a

mind of their own, and if you're not careful you could find yourself watching helplessly as trolley and human cargo crash through a barrier and disappear down a hole in the road or go hurtling through the plate-glass window of the nearest TV rental showroom. This could not only seriously damage the health of the passengers, it could also ruin the enjoyment of the crowd of Wallies on the pavement outside watching Celebrity Golf from Gleneagles.

Roadside picnicking

Like so many Wally activities, roadside picnicking is by no means as easy as it looks and should not be regarded as a form of recreation or relaxation.

One of the first problems you will have to contend with is that of struggling to erect recalcitrant picnic tables and folding stools while being buffeted by the tailwind from passing juggernauts. For the same reason, you're also going to have a devil of a job keeping that primus stove alight. A windbreak of the kind used on beaches can sometimes offer limited protection but it's often hard work trying to hammer the wooden stakes through four inches of unyielding tarmac.

Once your kettle has finally boiled, your tea has brewed and you've managed to unpack the tuna fish rolls from their layers of cling-film, you then face the problem of removing your oxygen mask for long enough to eat them while at the same time managing not to be overcome by exhaust fumes – which can be quite a feat of brinkmanship.

Ignore people who jeer at you from passing cars. They've probably never tried it themselves and haven't the faintest notion of the problems involved.

Two safety tips: always leave a margin of at least three feet between your picnic table and the nearest thundering oil tanker, and *don't* go in for brightly coloured tablecloths in jazzy designs that could startle motorists or flap around and get caught in the wheels of passing cars. This could cause a serious accident which could completely take away your appetite and even force you to abandon the picnic altogether. What's more, you'd never get the creases out of the tablecloth.

Where to picnic. Unfortunately, many of the really challenging and spectacular picnic spots are off-limits for one reason or another. The elevated section of the M4 is really just a bit too exposed for comfort – a sudden fierce gust of wind here could spell disaster, scattering your Ryvita and Primula cheese spread, and possibly you too, over half of Brentford. The same goes for the otherwise magnificent stretch of the M6 north of Junction 15 – with the additional hazard that thick fog mixed with diesel smoke from lorries grinding their way up that long incline can reduce visibility drastically and turn even the simplest task, such as finding your way to the liver sausage sandwiches or remembering where you put the picnic mustard, into a major trauma.

Large roundabouts, particularly if attractively landscaped and planted out with floral clocks, can make an ideal venue for a roadside picnic, and it's surprising that they're so little exploited by Wallies. However, if picnicking on a roundabout, do make sure you go fully prepared. There's nothing more frustrating than risking life and limb weaving your way through three fast-moving lines of traffic while laden down with chairs, table, primus stove and insulated picnic box, only to discover on arrival that you've forgotten the tin-opener.

Practice makes perfect. Like most high-visibility Wally activities, roadside picnicking should not be attempted until you're fully aware of all the potential risks and you're sure in your own mind that the project's not going to go off at half-cock, *i.e.* that you're *not* going to find yourself downwind of a Port-A-Loo used by gangs of Irish labourers in donkey jackets, or upstaged by a party of hitch-hikers or a hot-dog stand. You should also take precautions against being mistaken for a member of an avant-garde theatre group making a statement about environmental pollution and so get carted off by the police.

The best thing is to start modestly by practising in a car park – ideally an underground or multi-storey one where you're protected from the elements but also exposed to hefty doses of carbon monoxide. From there, work up to 'B' roads, building up confidence every time, until finally you're ready to tackle your first main roads and dual carriageways.

It will take time, but think of the rewards.

GET IT DOWN YOU

The Wally Good Drink Guide

Being a Wally can be extremely thirsty work, and after a hard day starting a forest fire or hogging the roundabouts in a children's playground, there's nothing more refreshing than to saunter into the Captain's Bar of the Moon and Parrot, order a pint of deliciously full-bodied Black Label, and chuck it over your best friend. He will then return the compliment by chucking one all over you, and before you know it everybody else will be joining in and the evening will have got off to a flying start.

Many novice Wallies make the elementary mistake of thinking that all you can do with drink is Get It Down you by the gallon. This is being very unimaginative. You can also Get It Down other people by pouring it over them from a tankard or spraying it at them out of a can (see p. 75). You can Bring It Up in interesting patterns either in the car park of the pub, on the pavement outside your local Pro Nuptia, or at home in your avocado vanity unit. And the following night as you return to the Moon and Parrot and set about going for the double, you can also Bring It Up Again – metaphorically this time, by entertaining friends or even total strangers with a blow-by-blow account of your antics the night before, going over the whole proceedings literally *ad nauseam*.

Before going on to discuss what to drink and where to drink, a few myths and common misconceptions about Wally drinking habits need to be discussed.

First, let's be clear about one thing. You shouldn't actually *need* strong alcoholic drink in order to go out and put the boot into a telephone box, wrap yourself round a lamp-post, or filch a collection of Road Up signs to decorate your bedroom. If you know your stuff you should be able to manage all those things quite comfortably on half a pint of Barbican. It's simply that because you're a Wally, you *like* the sensation of having six pints of lager, three whisky chasers and a couple of brandies for the road all slopping around in the pit of your stomach.

Secondly, it's not a good idea to pay too much attention to the killjoys who tell you that with every nip of own-brand supermarket Scotch, a million of your desperately needed brain cells will bite the dust. If you want to get the matter in perspective, remember that ten minutes' exposure to Good Morning Britain will probably dispose of at least twice as many – and for a fraction of the fun.

Most traditional drink guides approach the matter very much from the point of view of the drinker. But as we've seen, there are a number of other exciting things you can do with it as well. What follows, then, is a necessarily brief look at various tipples from the point of view of the drinker, pourer, chucker, sprayer and chunderer.

Beer. A vast range to choose from here, with many regional variations. Bear in mind, though, that the ones that get you in a window-smashing mood aren't always the ones with the best pouring or spraying properties – nor do they always give the best adhesion on lino floors. The best way to find the one that suits you is to experiment by chucking a wide selection, starting with the fizzy kegs and working your way steadily round to the dark, treacly Newcastle Browns, Old Peculiars and Winter Warmers at the other end of the spectrum. Stick with – if you'll forgive the pun – whichever one you feel most happy with. If you find you can stomach the taste too, you're home and dry – which is a great deal more than you can say for the people you've chucked it over.

A word here about the Campaign for Real Ale. CAMRA is chocker with Wallies, as you'd expect, and certainly if you're not a Wally when you join, by the time you've met the other members, developed a florid complexion and giant beer gut and spent a few evenings discussing the specific gravity of obscure West Country bitters while lying horizontal on the sawdust strewn floor of a Real Ale pub, you very soon will be.

However, not all Wallies are die-hard Real Ale enthusiasts by any means. Many feel that if you're going to drink beer that's flat, cloudy and has lots of unsavoury-looking bits floating in it, the proper thing to do is to save yourself a few pennies and brew it yourself.

Lager. Lager is the Wally drink *par excellence*, but choosing the right brand from all the Heinekens, Hemelings, Carlings, Stellas and so on can be a real problem. The ads don't help here. Amongst all those tankards bursting out of blocks of ice in slow motion, humanoid bears relaxing at the local and ordering drinks all round, and rugged-looking types in denim shirts striding purposefully across sun-parched deserts, there's not one that tells the Wally punter what he wants to know about the product, *i.e.* what harmful chemical additives does it contain? How long has it been kept festering in a plastic vat? Will it do lasting damage to your insides? And so on.

Perhaps the marketing men are afraid that if they revealed that it wasn't brewed in steaming wooden tubs by Vikings but by spotty little men in white coats in places like Slough, they'd lose sales. If so, one can only say that they sadly underestimate the brand loyalty of Joe Wally down at the Moon and Parrot.

If you want to be a discerning Wally drinker, don't allow sophisticated television advertising campaigns to interfere with your choice of lager. Just work your way systematically through the major brands until you find the one that makes you burp the loudest and tastes most reminiscent of chilled horse pee.

Sherry. Not a drink for any Wally concerned with establishing his credibility among his mates. This is the kind of drink your bank manager might offer you before refusing your request for extended overdraft facilities. Buy your girl-friend a Sweet Sherry as an aperitif in a Berni, but otherwise avoid.

Wines and spirits. Lack of volume and expense are the two main drawbacks here, so there isn't much you can do with either type except drink them — which makes them dull for the Wally. The trouble is, they come in such miserable little glasses. Chucking a gin and tonic down the back of someone's neck may be a good laugh, but at upwards of 90p a time it's certainly not a cheap one. Also, in order to produce any kind of satisfactory reaction you're going to have to jettison the whole glass, gin, tonic, ice and lemon and all. You could theoretically just give your victim the ice and the tonic and retain the rest, but it could earn you a reputation for being stingy, especially when other Wallies are slopping pints around.

Another drawback is that few wines and spirits can be shaken up in the bottle and squirted. The only fizzy drinks in this line are the sparkling whites, the Lambruscos and the Champagnes, and since there's nothing you can do with any of them that you can't do just as enjoyably and effectively with a can of Skol, it seems pointless going to all that extra expense – on top of which, people might think you were being ostentatious.

Soft drinks. Certain drinks become Wally when sprayed over passersby; others are intrinsically Wally even before they leave the can. In other cases, such as Coke, Wally status isn't fully assured until the empty can has been dropped into someone's front garden or run over by a car. The following, however, can be sipped out of the finest crystal goblets and will still be Wally: Fanta (any flavour), Dr Pepper, Schweppes Cariba, Top Deck Lemonade Shandy, Seven-Up, Pineapple and Grapefruit Lilt, Tizer, Corona, Robinson's Passionade, Diet Pepsi, Bingo Cola.

Drinks for the Harlow Harpie and other female Wallies. The female Wally has an exasperating fondness for exotic and usually expensive concoctions such as Ponies, Snowballs, White Ladies, Crocodillos, Riccadonnas, Rum and blackcurrant, Creme de Menthe, Port and lemonade, Campari and soda – although you may be lucky and find one who drinks nothing but Slimline tonic.

Be warned: cocktails are also a favourite. Many Wally pubs have a so-called Happy Hour when you can buy them at half-price, but they're still not exactly cheap. If you can shell out a fiver on a round of Pinacoladas and Harvey

Wallbangers and manage to look happy, have no fear —
you're definitely a Wally.

Where to drink – the Wally Pub Guide

Choosing the right pub is crucial. There's nothing worse
than striding confidently into what you imagine to be a
Wally pub only to find yourself surrounded by bearded
Radio Three listeners earnestly discussing late Bartok,
trendies in granny specs and fisherman's smocks reviving
ancient and deservedly neglected pub games from the Black
Country, and finger-in-the-ear folk singers wearing Arran
sweaters or sheepskin jerkins performing incomprehensible
songs about obscure mining disasters. It's bad enough when
you're on your own: it's potentially disastrous if you're with
a group of other Wallies who up till now have respected you
for your general taste and discernment. Bang goes your
Wally credibility.

There are pubs for folkies and domino-players, and there
are pubs for people like you. You stay off their patch, they'll
stay off yours. The rule is: only drink in Wally pubs, *unless*
(a) you are deliberately venturing into non-Wally territory
in order to conduct some kind of public relations exercise on
behalf of Wallies, such as a demonstration of beer-chucking,
crisp-packet bursting or peanut-juggling; or (b) you are in
possession of a six-pack of Heineken or some such, in which
case you are free to drink more or less anywhere you like.
In fact, the more imaginative your choice of location the
better. *Don't* just sit at home and swill it down in front of
The Professionals — take a couple of cans and experiment
with different venues: squatting on the pavement outside
Sainsbury's; stretched out on a gravestone; or if you can
afford it, sprawled across four seats of a British Airways
passenger flight to Malta.

How to find a Wally pub. Experienced Wallies can sniff out
Wally pubs in the most unlikely places. You'll find it harder
to begin with. Basically, though, it's not so much a question
of where to look as of what to look for. To avoid making

embarrassing mistakes which could lead your friends to question your nous and put unnecessary strain on your bottle, give any likely-looking pub a brief once-over first, asking yourself the following questions:

1) Does it contain a huge Alsatian fed on dropped crisps and half-eaten ploughman's lunches?

2) Does it offer the very latest in pub entertainment? (*I.e.*, table video games: Asteroids, Astro-Blasters, Space Invaders; a jukebox that plays The Human League an average of fifteen times per session; Friday night guest appearances by Country and Western artistes who, according to the poster, have appeared regularly on TV but who in fact have never appeared regularly anywhere except in the Engagements Wanted columns of the *Melody Maker*.)

3) Does it contain blackened roof timbers bearing the sign 'Duck or Grouse'?

4) Are the toilets labelled 'Guys and Dolls', 'Cocks and Hens', 'Actresses and Bishops', or 'Lords and Ladies'?

5) Are the walls of the Gents covered with graffiti painstakingly copied from paperbacks by Nigel Rees? Does it also contain a contraceptive machine on which someone has scribbled 'Buy me and stop one' or 'This chewing gum tastes revolting'?

6) Is there a parrot or minah bird behind the bar that squawks 'Time, gentlemen, please'?

While you're at it, it's also worth finding out — assuming it's not abundantly clear already — whether or not the landlord is a Wally too. The Wally landlord usually exhibits the following characteristics:

1) He is a former heavyweight boxing coach or record producer who has worked with all the big names in the business.

2) He sucks up to members of the local constabulary by inviting them to discreet naughty-naughty after-hours drinking sessions with the regulars.

74

The Wally Step by Step Guide to Drinking from Ring-Pull Cans

1 Agitate can vigorously.

2 Open, taking care to direct jet of froth over fellow Wallies or passers-by. (see inset)

3 Drain in one.

4 Belch.

5 Mangle.

6 Chuck.

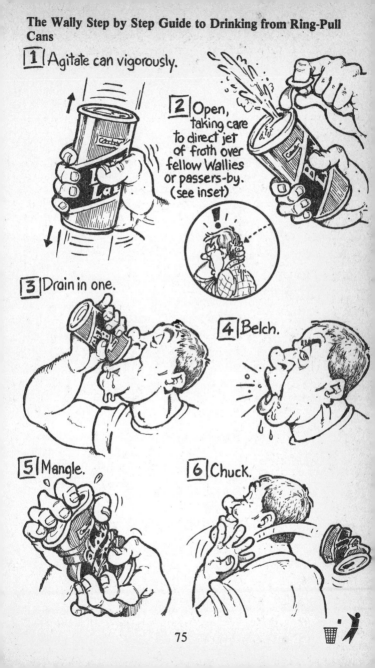

3) He sends departing patrons on their way with a cheery 'Don't forget the seat belts'.

4) He not only welcomes passing trade in the form of parties of middle-aged ladies in crimplene trouser suits and cowboy hats; he lies down in the middle of the road in the path of oncoming coaches and implores them to pull in and taste his internationally famous bar snacks.

5) He festoons the walls with postcards sent by regulars holidaying in Majorca and photographs bearing warm messages of friendship from (a) famous people he crawled to in his heavyweight boxing or record-producing days, or (b) hapless celebrities who once made the mistake of sneaking into his pub to use the toilets and found they couldn't get back to their car without signing autographs and buying drinks all round.

Wally pub grub

There are strict rules governing the serving of food and bar snacks in Wally pubs and it's up to you as a Wally consumer to see that standards are maintained. Don't buy food from pubs where the following rules are not observed:

1) Practically everything except soup should be served in a basket.

2) Where possible, food should induce halitosis. Salads should be heavy on the spring onions and ploughman's lunches should always be accompanied by more Branston pickle, piccallilli and pickled onions and cocktail gherkins than anyone except a bad-breath fanatic would want to eat.

3) Sandwiches should be left to mature in the kitchens for several days and allowed to make their own way to the food counter, where they should then be garnished with a sprig of fresh parsley and smothered in Clingfilm.

4) All bar and kitchen staff should be issued with Photofit pictures of Egon Ronay and local Department of Health inspectors and trained in case of emergency to

activate a self-destruct mechanism concealed beneath the food counter.

5) Pub diners who make a nuisance of themselves by changing their order at the last minute or losing their cloakroom ticket should either be verbally ridiculed in front of other customers or have soup spilt down them.

6) Quiche Lorraine, if available, should be referred to on the menu as 'flan'. pie

7) Items of confectionery should be on sale behind the bar. Crisps should be available in as many outlandish flavours as possible – Roast Ox, Prawn Cocktail, Barbecued Piranha Fish – but never the one you actually ask for.

8) All Scotch eggs should contain a gap of approx. 1/8 in. between the egg and the sausage meat, and the breadcrumbs should on no account be crisp.

THE W-PLAN DIET

If you want to be a Wally, you've got to eat like a Wally.

There's no way you can seriously contemplate a busy day's welly-chucking or poster defacement on a meagre diet of starch-reduced crispbread, unsweetened orange juice, black coffee and the odd slice of raw carrot. You need something considerably more substantial.

What you need is the W-Plan Diet.

The W-Plan Diet consists of solid, no-nonsense, no-nutritional-value junk food that catapults you straight into the coronary high-risk bracket and will have you wearing false teeth by thirty.

The W-Plan Diet is tailor-made to meet the varied needs of today's busy go-anywhere perpetual-motion Wally. It doesn't involve boring calorie charts and long lists of dietary dos and don'ts; it doesn't require you to gulp down huge quantities of grapefruit with every meal or make a complete social leper of yourself by living only on All Bran or rabbit food. With the W-Plan Diet you eat what you like, where you like, when you like: Benson's Kingsnax, Planter's Peanuts, French bread pizzas, chip butties, Angel Delight, whatever you fancy – so long as it comes in a brightly coloured wrapper, you can stuff it down you.

Flexibility is the keynote. Instead of laying down the law about what you can and can't eat, the W-Plan Diet is *realistic* about your eating habits. It recognises that there may be times when you have no choice but to eat a slice of wholemeal bread. It says: if you *have* to, go ahead – but at least try and kill the taste by spreading it with Ham and Cheese Toasties, or cancel out the effect by having an extra helping of Alphabetti Spaghetti later in the day.

There are really only two rules you should bear in mind when following the W-Plan Diet.

1) If you have to cook food yourself, at least keep preparation time to a minimum. As a Wally, you've got better things to do than sit in your knotty-pine kitchen with your eyes glued to an oven-timer. Stick to foods that

you can boil in the bag, bung in a microwave oven or serve simply by adding hot water.

2) Try and eat your meals with the telly on. This applies particularly to breakfast. Even devilled kidneys and kedgeree can be part of your W-Plan Diet if you eat them while watching Breakfast Television.

W-Plan menus for special occasions

Choosing the right menu for that intimate soiree can be something of a problem, not only for beginners but even for the veteran Wally host and hostess. What dishes are and are not Wally?

The answer very much depends on the way they're prepared and served and the exact circumstances in which they're eaten. Braised duckling with olives served with new potatoes, artichoke hearts and a side-salad is not exactly traditional Wally fare – but you could make it acceptable if you drowned it in brown sauce and expected your guests to shovel it down with a couple of slices of Mother's Pride and a cup of PG Tips while watching Crossroads. Similarly, Gateau Mille Feuilles au Citron: not an item gracing many Wally dinner tables – but you might just smuggle it past an undiscerning palate if it was cunningly smothered in tinned custard or Bird's Dream Topping.

Other cases are even less clear-cut. Caviare, for example. Could it be Wally if you served it in a toasted sandwich? Would Chocolate Bath Oliver biscuits be Wally if you got a free voucher with every tin entitling you to send away for a cut-price Swiss Army pen-knife? Hard to say.

What *is* clear is that initially at least, success as a Wally chef depends on going by the book and avoiding risky flights of culinary fancy until you've mastered the basics. More experienced Wally cooks can take even the most unappetising-sounding dishes and transform them into something really special: tasting their Moussaka or Baked Alaska you'd almost swear you were eating a Fray Bentos steak and kidney pie or a shop-bought Arctic Roll. For you, it's more important to concentrate on simple menus. Try and remember too those little details that are so vital to successful Wally cuisine. There's nothing more discouraging than to go to endless trouble preparing a slap-up banquet consisting of frankfurters in brine and a dollop of Smash followed by fruit cocktail and Ideal milk, only to see the entire evening ruined because you failed to bring on the Branston or make with the after-dinner mints.

Enlivening your W-Plan Diet

One exciting way to inject variety into your diet is to try eating out at home once in a while. It sounds like a contradiction in terms, but it *can* be done if you follow the instructions and sample menus set out below.

The Stay-At-Home British Airways In-Flight Ham Salad Banquet for 1. Holidays come all too rarely – so why not relive all the excitement of starting out on a two-week package tour of the Costa Brava, only this time without setting foot outside your own front door?

Simply draw the curtains of your lounge-diner, litter the room with mementos of the trip or screen some holiday home movies to get yourself in the mood, then strap yourself into your Parker Knoll recliner – and it's chocks away!

Without waiting for smoking or seatbelt restrictions to be lifted, pour yourself a plastic tumbler of Bacardi, tear open a carton of those duty-free Winstons you put by specially for the occasion and light up. While a friend or loved one violently agitates your easy chair to simulate in-flight turbulence, tuck into those glistening squares of processed ham, tired-looking lettuce leaves, cocktail gherkins, Jacob's Cream Crackers with squidgy semi-melted butter, and jellied pears with angelica on the top. Round off your meal by spilling scalding hot coffee in your lap as your companion announces that due to a strike by Spanish air traffic controllers your flight has been diverted to Zurich.

Variation: As above, except that you simulate the return flight. This involves less outlay on food: you're suffering from gastro-enteritis and all you can eat are Cream Crackers.

The Stay-At-Home Berni Inn on Cup Final Night Special. However much you'd like to, it's just not possible to dine at a Berni Inn every night of the week. So once in a while why not do the next best thing and try and recreate that unique Berni ambience in your own front room? It's cheap, easy – and if you're going all out for authenticity, you could even arrange for a group of your Wally friends to burst in halfway through the meal and impersonate a jubilant horde of victorious Manchester United fans chucking bread rolls and yelling for service.

Prepare the scene by spreading red chequered tablecloths over everything in sight and pour a brimming tankard of Black Label for yourself and a huge schooner of sweet sherry for your female companion while the two of you study the menu. One of you should then take the role of waiter or waitress, while the other, after hours of thought, finally opts with devastating originality for prawn cocktail followed by steak and chips; whoever is acting the customer then has all the fun of sending back the steak when it arrives either toasted to a crisp or stone cold in the middle. As fitting end to a perfect evening, you should then stage a pointless argument over the bill and storm out, having first filled your pockets with bread rolls and miniature packs of butter, leaving the waiter/waitress to be roasted on a spit by those Manchester United fans who are not already fully occupied performing Tommy Cooper tricks with the tablecloths.

The Stay-At-Home Motorway Service Station breakfast. As any true Wally will tell you, there's nothing quite like staggering red-eyed with exhaustion into the Watford Gap Services after six hours' night driving and tucking into a high-cholesterol breakfast of chips, beans, fried egg and bacon and toast and jam, especially when you can eat within earshot of the Space Invaders and relax to the sound of a heavy metal band and their road crew, fresh from a gig, thrashing hell out of a pinball machine outside – and that's the experience you can recreate in your own home thanks to this unique Wally Stay-At-Home.

Simply stock up in advance with plastic tubs of butter

and jam and cook all food the previous night. Leave to stew overnight on a hostess trolley; then in the morning invite a party of headbangers or long-distance lorry drivers to share it with you, tempting them with the prospect of free access to your huge stock of Atari video games or a chance to scatter your specially procured soiled paper hand towels all over the bathroom.

CHEZ WALLY

Being a Wally doesn't end when you come home in the evening, shut the front door behind you and slump down in front of the telly. It's an all-embracing life-style – and that means that your home should be Wally too. Imagine how shaming it would be, for instance, to invite a few of your Wally friends back to your home for a mug of banana Nesquick and a Rich Tea biscuit after a night at the pub, and have to usher them into a house full of stripped pine and glass-mounted National Theatre posters! Spare yourself a few blushes and muttered apologies by making sure that your home unambiguously reflects your status as a Wally. Follow the advice in this section and you won't put a foot wrong.

Wally-Plan

When it comes to furnishing your home, there's no room for half measures. Avoid at all costs the type of decorative and aesthetic gaffes so many novice Wallies are prone to: the careless juxtaposition of a Habitat table lamp with a set of walnut veneer nesting tables from John Lewis; the ghastly blunder of scattering poncy floral cushions from Laura Ashley all over your Times Furnishing settee. Lesson Number One is: have the courage of your convictions. Be a Wally – and let your surroundings prove you're one.

Take the lounge, for example. *Don't* waste time, energy and money commissioning a firm of interior decorators to create for you a dynamic split-level living environment consisting of acres of white wool carpet and tubular steel furniture with the pipe work and electricity cables daringly exposed. Don't muck it up by going for shrill primary colours, natural wood or Abyssinian wall-hangings. All you want in your lounge is space in which to put up your Steve Davis Fold-Away Mini-Snooker table and congenial surroundings in which to bash out a tune a day on the home organ, kick the cat, bolt down a TV dinner, mix yourself a drink at the bar and possibly ask a few friends round for a screening of your Task Force Special tapes on the video. You require, in short, a room in which you can open a Watney's Party Four without fear of causing irreparable damage to a priceless Henry Moore lithograph – and you definitely want those pipes and cables out of sight so that you can whack a nail through them when you come to hang a picture.

Textiles. In Wally homes, practical and aesthetic considerations should go hand in hand. Carpets, for example, should be of man-made fibre in swirling multi-coloured designs so that fag ends, crisps, half-eaten Jammie Dodgers and anything else that doesn't get gobbled up by the Alsatian can be trodden in without leaving a trace. Sofas and chairs should be upholstered in wipe-clean leatherette for similar sound practical reasons. And wall surfaces should be heavily textured, either with flock wallpapers, anaglyptas or Sandtex Fine Build, so that when the odd plateful of Vesta Beef Curry or take-away Chinese goes flying across the room and gets stuck to the wall it can pass more or less unnoticed.

Patterns and colour schemes. Your only purely aesthetic foible should concern stripes. Bold stripes in bright colours belong on cars, toothpaste and down the sleeves of anoraks – not on walls. Beyond that, you should refuse to be fettered by conventional notions about clashing patterns or the inadvisability of combining chintz with tartan and polka dots. If you hit on a combination that makes your eyes water and evokes either Carnival Week in Rio or Mardi Gras in New Orleans, you'll know you're on the right lines.

Colour can be a problem area for the Wally home furnisher, mainly because your ideas are liable to be heavily conditioned by the kind of milk-and-water schemes you've seen in magazines like *Homes and Gardens*, where the major aim is to provide a muted background for those rows and rows of unread Penguins with their vivid orange spines. Your first step in choosing a colour scheme is to clear your mind of these pernicious influences. Remember: Wallies do not make 'statements' in gentle pastel shades, nor do they use cunning colour contrasts in order to create a feeling of space or to bring the walls in closer or the ceiling down lower. If you want to lower a ceiling, the way to do it is to puncture a waterbed or leave the taps running on the floor above.

Further, the kind of statements you want to make in your home cannot be made with conventional colours such as Magnolia, Honeysuckle, Oyster or Dusky Pink; they have to be made with the following range of Wally-Plan Specials:

- Sour Cream
- Rosy Nipple
- Thames Mud
- Snot green
- Branston Pickle
- Scarlet Fever
- Caramel Custard
- Channel Grey
- Cow Pat
- Hot Flush
- Danish Blue
- Piccallilli
- Bladderwrack
- Curious Yellow
- Tabasco
- Mushy Pea

Also, if you *have* to choose one of those subtle 'White? Not Quite' shades, make it one of the following: Slightly Soiled, Deathly Pale, or Top of the Milk.

Furniture. No hard and fast rules here. Go for robustness and durability obviously, but not at the expense of unsightliness. Don't be fooled into buying supposedly 'period' furniture which has been artificially aged in a repro workshop. If anyone's going to put ring marks, scratches, dents, chips and inkstains all over your furniture, it should be you.

Ornaments and decorative items. The key word here is 'overkill'. Don't make the mistake of decorating your G-Plan sideboard with a single tasteful spray of 'Soft Silk' washable fabric flowers and expect to score points for showing classic restraint and decorum. Your miserliness with the knick-knacks will simply allow your friends to indulge the suspicion that you're not fully conversant with the range of Wally ornaments and that the washable flowers were a fluke. They could even draw the conclusion that you didn't choose them yourself at all, but had them given to you by a friend and that secretly you hate the sight of them.

To be absolutely sure of creating the right impression, fill every corner of your home with all of the following:

- Framed colour prints of Alpine scenes
- Caithness glass paperweights
- Shakespearian 'character' jugs
- Handpainted stoneware rabbits, unicorns and field birds
- Royal Doulton 'Bunnykins' figurines
- Decorative herb sachets in the form of owls, cats, etc.
- Wax candles in the form of fruit and vegetables
- Miniature bone china wheelbarrows full of flowers
- Raffia-bound Chianti bottles or leather Sangria decanters
- Porcelain figures of Victorian Nannies, Old Sea Dogs, Pirates, Mr Pickwick, Huckleberry Finn and Winston Churchill
- Crocheted lavatory-roll holders in the form of poodles
- Flamenco dolls
- Tretchikoff and David Shepherd prints
- Photographs of yourself in Victorian or Wild West costume
- Glass bells and engraved Regency brandy-snifters
- Bullfight posters with your name printed in place of the matador's
- Ivory and bronze figures of Ian Botham, Dennis Lillee etc. in the 'Arlott's Immortals' series
- Shimmering fibre-optic whatsits
- Cylindrical illuminated thingummies
  (See also *How to buy a sumptuous hand-crafted Objet d'Art*, p. 60)

The Wally Guide to Do It Yourself

When it comes to the actual fabric of your home, you could be lucky and find yourself living in a house that already has ill-fitting doors, paper-thin walls, 4-inch soil pipes running through the lounge and light switches put on at peculiar angles. On the other hand, you could find that you have to add these essential features yourself, by slaving away with a Black and Decker in your spare evenings and at weekends. Usually, though, even if your house *was* either jerrybuilt originally or extensively botched up by a previous owner, you will still wish to add some little touches of your own, simply to imprint your personality on it. You could be ambitious and transform the exterior in the manner shown in the diagram on p. 91. Or you could just add features such as a home sauna, a bar in the lounge, Wild West saloon doors, a handsome brick fireplace surround or simply a little porcelain sign on the loo door saying '*Yer Tiz*'.

The only proper way to go about these tasks is to Do Them Yourself. As a Wally, you should in any case be a DIY fanatic, for the following reasons:

1) DIY is manly and nous-intensive and gives you an excuse to wear grubby overalls, carry a steel tape measure in your pocket, stick ciggies and stubs of pencil behind your ear, and for once in your life look as if you know what you're doing.
2) DIY affords endless opportunities to fall off ladders, get splinters in your bottom, slice the top off your fingers, get your head stuck in buckets and electrocute yourself – all under the pretext of doing useful jobs about the house.
3) DIY enables you not only to embellish your own home with louvre doors and polystyrene ceiling tiles from MFI, but also, when visiting friends' houses, to go around pointing out cracks in the plaster and patches of dry rot and woodworm, prodding the walls with your pocket Dampometer, tut-tutting, shaking your head gloomily, whistling through your teeth and generally volunteering vast amounts of unwanted advice.

Wally DIY should not be confused with conventional DIY. Conventional DIY is easy. All you have to do is make sure you've got the right tools to hand, estimate materials sensibly and set about each job methodically. Wally DIY is hard — and it's still hard even when you know how. To begin with, it calls for a number of skills which you're *not* going to pick up from the Reader's Digest *Book of the Home*: the skill of guiding a power-saw while simultaneously hand-rolling a cigarette and reading your horoscope in the *Daily Mirror*; wiring up an extra spur on the ring main with the power on; wriggling your way under the floorboards while holding a lighted match in order to check for gas leaks; that special knack of demolishing load-bearing walls without being crushed to death by an avalanche of falling masonry. There are some jobs, frankly, that turn out to be beyond the scope of even the most enthusiastic Wally DIY-er; in such cases, all you can do is swallow your pride and call in a firm of cowboys to do the job for you.

Building an extension to your home. This can not only greatly enlarge your living space and add a whole new dimension to your home, it can also be a very useful way of using up all the polystyrene ceiling tiles and louvre doors you over-ordered on your last DIY project. An extension with a flat felt roof covered with gravel chippings also makes an excellent outdoor cat litter.

The conventional way to go about building an extension is to start with the foundations and work your way upwards, leaving the roof till last. This isn't by any means the only method, but it does at least have the virtue of allowing you to tackle the most enjoyable bit first. This is where you recreate a First World War battle-scene in your back garden by stripping to the waist, marching out into the pouring rain, digging down through four feet of solid clay, putting a pickaxe through the mains drainage channel and catching either pneumonia or Trench Foot. The other advantage is that should you discover at this early stage that your garden has a high water table, *i.e.* floods of water lying inches below the surface, there's still time to abandon

Before ...

After ...

91

your scheme for an extension and think about a swimming pool instead.

Work in progress. Whatever project you decide on, whether it's a pool, a granny annexe for the wife and kids or a multi-level sun patio consisting of acres of pink and yellow crazy paving, perforated concrete balustrades, plastic birdbaths and floodlit fountains, don't forget to keep a complete step-by-step photographic record of the building work with which to bore the pants off your friends at social gatherings. This should be in the form of an imitation leather photo album containing pictures of you (1) ceremonially cutting the first sod or taking the first wild swing with a sledgehammer; (2) giving a cheerful thumbs-up to the camera, blissfully unaware that the concrete lintel above your head is about to give away, burying you under a couple of tons of breeze-blocks; (3) grinning ruefully as you attempt to extract your wellies from six inches of quick-setting ready-mix concrete; (4) reversing a hired mechanical digger into your next-door neighbour's garden fence; and finally (5) proudly glueing the last strip of woodgrain laminate or polystyrene ceiling tile in position while perched precariously on the top of a step ladder.

With each project you tackle, your collection of photo albums should grow, until eventually they take up so much room in your home that you have to build a special photo album extension to accomodate them. You will then be able to record the building of the photo album extension in an especially lavish photo album extension album.

Painting and decorating. Wall-papering and painting are well within the scope of the Wally DIY enthusiast, and it requires surprisingly little effort to make a really spectacular pig's dinner of both. In fact, hanging a strip of wall-paper crooked or upside down, or so that the pattern doesn't match up is *so* easy that in order to do it you don't really have to be a Wally at all — which is bound to take away somewhat from the satisfaction you'll feel with the end result.

Painting, too, is made almost *too* easy for you by the fact that so often the paint inside the tin bears no relation at all to the colour on the lid or chart. It's therefore as easy to hit on a Wally colour scheme by accident as to sit down for hours with a set of colour charts and really work at it.

Take care to prepare all surfaces properly before you start painting. There are several proprietary paint strippers on the market that do an excellent job of removing layers of human skin but few that work as well on layers of old paint. If you have a large area of old paint you want stripped, eat a garlic mayonnaise burger and six packets of cheese and onion crisps and try breathing on it.

Energy-saving in the home. Never waste money by allowing precious heat to escape through your roof or through draughty windows or doors. Instead, waste money by installing costly and ineffective double-glazing.

WALLIES SANS FRONTIERES

The Wally Holiday Guide

The holiday season begins early these days. To be exact, it begins as you sit in a post-Christmas daze, gazing blankly at the second commercial break in the annual Boxing Day screening of The Sound of Music (the first commercial break having been entirely given over to ads announcing fabulous reductions and sale bargains at Debenham's). Dimly you perceive through a swirling haze of Henri Winterman smoke and Creme de Menthe fumes that the bikini-clad girl waving at you from a speedboat in Torremolinos is altogether too generously endowed to be Julie Andrews. Then realisation dawns. What you're watching isn't The Sound of Music at all. It's the first holiday ad of the year — which means that the time has come once more to think about booking up for your annual dose of instant sunburn and foreign tummy ...

Being a Wally holidaymaker used to be easy. All you had to do was go on a package holiday to Benidorm and spend a fortnight cheek by jowl with hordes of pleasure-seekers from Birmingham and Wolverhampton, stuffing your face with paiella and chips and manfully lending a hand with the building work on your hotel. Nowadays it's not so simple. The problem is, there just aren't enough half-finished Spanish holiday hotels to go round any more. Another problem is that a hundred and one equally enticing Wally-traps also beckon, every one of them bristling with Kojak bars, Travolta discos, British pubs serving fizzy keg beers and nightclubs offering superb evening entertainment by top European Cabaret Artistes.

So where do you go these days if you want Delhi Belly but you don't want to go to India for it?

The answer is that you don't have to go anywhere. A perfectly acceptable Wally holiday is simply to steam aimlessly back and forth across the English Channel, drinking yourself blind on duty-free booze and falling down the companionways. You could also take the advice contained in the Wally caravanning guide and stick to the British Isles, enjoying some of the splendid hold-ups and tailbacks listen on pp. 104-6. But if you are intent on going abroad and giving the locals a free course of instruction in how to be a Wally and you don't know which resort to choose, there's one rule of thumb you can always apply. Instead of wasting hours poring over travel brochures, simply ask yourself, Is it the kind of place where Bobby Moore might open a nightclub? If the answer's yes, it's safe to go ahead and book up. But *hurry*.

Planning your Wally package holiday

The success of your Wally package holiday depends to a great extent on luck. There are always the thousand-to-one-against disasters that no amount of careful planning can forestall: for instance, you might be travelling economy class to Tenerife and find yourself engaged in conversation by an international lawyer or surrounded by a party of nuns. You could book a holiday in Malta and find when you got there that by some extraordinary freak you'd hit on the one time of year when there wasn't another English tourist in sight. You could just be cracking a tube of lager on the back seat of your Cosmos Tourama coach when you discover that by some administrative blunder you've been assigned to a tour that involves being rudely dragged out of the coach at intervals and forced to footslog it round art galleries, museums and ancient monuments ...

Equally, there are always the unexpected bonuses. You might for instance time your holiday to coincide with a baggagehandlers' strike or a work to rule by port officials, and end up spending an unforgettable week camping in an airport departure lounge or sunning yourself on the quayside at Dover. It's swings and roundabouts all the way with holidays.

However, between the two extremes of the unexpected boons and the unexpected disasters, there's a vast amount that you can achieve by planning. Do your best to ensure that your Wally Continental package includes at least one of the following essential ingredients.

Overbooking. Remember the famous state-room scene in the Marx Brothers' A Night At The Opera? Aim for the same scenes of mayhem and confusion on board your plane or ship or on arrival at your holiday hotel or villa. Method: place all booking arrangements in the hands of one of the less reputable tour operators and they'll take care of everything.

A six-hour wait at Luton airport. Is it possible to get *anywhere* from Luton airport? Find out the hard way. Guaranteed to get your holiday off to a flying start eventually.

Lost luggage. You spend two weeks in Lido di Jesolo in the clothes you stand up in. Your luggage has the holiday of a lifetime in Honolulu. Simple to arrange: some airlines do it as a matter of course.

Sunburn. The Lobster Look renders you immediately recognisable as a Wally and avoids any risk of you being mistaken for a run-of-the-mill holidaymaker. Method: one way is to motor down to the Algarve in one hop, strip off on arrival and flop down in an exhausted heap in a fierce sun for a few hours. Practise by falling asleep under your sun-ray lamp.

Holiday tummy. Comes in two forms. There's no need to miss out by only going down with one of them; simply exceed the stated Senakot dose and you'll have a full house.

Useful Phrases for Continental Holidays

Out and about

Can you direct me to the nearest bar serving lukewarm Barbican?

Pouvez-vous me diriger au bar le plus proche servant de la Barbican tiède?

Pueded dirigirme al bar más cercano dénde sirven Barbican templado?

My pedal boat has been struck by a freak tidal wave.

Mon pedale-bateau été frappé par une vague de fond capricieuse.

Un maremoto extraordinario ha volcado mi patin.

This square foot of beach is already taken.

Ce pied carré de la plage a été pris déjà.

Este metro quadrado de playa ya está ocupado.

The fat German from Room 903 has just spontaneously combusted by the poolside.

Le gros allemand dans la chambre numero 903 a spontanément combusté au bord de la piscine.

El alemán gordo de la habitacion 903 hacaba de estallar en llamas espontaniamente al lado de la piscina.

At the police

My St Christopher medallion became entangled with this young lady's belt buckle at a Club Wally beach barbecue.

Mon medaillon St Christophe s'est entanglé avec la ceinture de cette jeune fille au barbecue du Club Wally.

Mi medalla de S. Cristóbal se enredo con la hebilla de su cinturón en la barbacoa playera del Club Wally.

I only wanted one as a souvenir.

Je le voulais seulement comme souvenir.

Solo queria uno como recuerdo.

In the restuarant

I have got my head stuck in an ice bucket.

J'ai coincé ma tête dans le seau à glaçons.

Tengo mi cabeza atascada en un cubo de hielo.

97

I seem to have left my American Express card in the Cortina.
Il semble que j'ai oublié ma carte American Express dans la Cortina.
Me parece que me he dejado mi tarjeta del American Express en el Cortina.

When I want Ambre Solaire on my salad, I'll ask for it, thank you.
Quand j'aurai besoin d'une vinaigrette à l'Ambre Solaire, je vous la demanderai, merci.
Cuando quiera Ambre Solaire en mi ensalata, se lo pediré, gracias.

At the disco

Come outside and say that.
Venez dehors et répétez cela.
Sal a fuera a decirmelo.

At the doctor's

And the next thing I knew, he stuck one on me.
Et tout à coup, il m'en a collé un.
A continuación, lo que pasó es que me pegó una.

I have scorched my upper lip on a glass of flaming Sambucca.
J'ai brûlé ma lèvre supérieure avec un verre de Sambucca flambant.
Me he quemado el labio superior con un vaso de Zambucca quemante.

I have been struck on the epiglotis by a frisbee.
Mon épiglotte a été heurtée par un frisbi.
Me han dado en la epiglotis con un frisbee.

My friend has a pink cocktail parasol lodged in his windpipe.
Mon ami a un parasole rose de cocktail coincé dans son gosier.
Mi amigo tiene un parasolillo de coctel de color rosa atascado en la trachea.

At the boutique

I'll take the one with the Go Faster stripes.
Je prends celle avec les rayures de vitesse.
Me quedo el que tiene las correas de velocidad.

At the customs

I swear to God I've never seen them before in my life.
Je jure devant Dieu, Monsieur l'inspecteur douanier, que je ne les ai jamais vu de ma vie.
Se lo juro por Dios que no las he visto en mi vida.

The Wally Guide to Holiday Activities on the Continent

Simply by choosing to take a holiday in a place like Marbella or Ostend you will already have given evidence to suggest that you are a Wally. But of course it doesn't end there.

While abroad, it is your duty to demonstrate your skills to the local residents and to prove to them that when it comes to being a Wally, the British can still teach the world a thing or two. You can do this in a number of ways, ranging from simply failing to observe the most elementary hygeine and safety precautions to performing acts of bravado or daring abandon such as leaping on to the table in a Spanish nightclub with a rose clenched between your teeth and flamenco-dancing in your underpants or conducting mock bull-fights using tablecloths and a sweet trolley. More suggestions are given below.

Being a Wally on the Continent means hard work and long hours, often for very little reward other than the occasional volley of derision from other holidaymakers and the water-cannon, CS gas or rubber truncheon treatment from local police or paramilitaries. But don't be too downcast if you have to spend a few days picking cockroaches out of your soup in a sweltering lockup somewhere on the Costa del Sol. Remember: if enough other Wallies follow your example, the message will eventually get through to your host nation. And think of the satisfaction you'll feel when hordes of Spanish Wallies come pouring off the ferry at Southampton, wearing plastic Union Jack bowlers and blowing whoopee whistles, and set about laying waste to the south of England.

Defacing or chipping pieces off ancient monuments. If you are ever unfortunate enough to find yourself whisked off against your will and forced to gawp admiringly at ancient relics, one way to make the experience just about bearable is to carve your initials all over the monuments in question or break off a chunk to take home to show your friends. Try to get in a bit of practice before you go abroad by spraying Wallies Rule OK all over Stonehenge with a blue aerosol. The famous figure of Winged Victory in the Louvre with both arms missing shows what you can achieve if you put your mind to it.

Causing an affray in nightclubs and discos. Don't leave it all to the professional footballers and the sailors on shore leave. Build up gradually to a fully-fledged brawl by persistently shouting for the band to play 'Una Paloma Blanca', 'Viva Espana' or 'The Birdy Song' and chanting or slow-handclapping through the cabaret. Then needle the locals by taking to the stage yourself, drink in hand, singing a chorus of 'Roll Out The Barrel', making jocular reference to the Spanish Armada, the bloody nose we Brits gave the French at Agincourt, the Italian book of War Heroes, or touching on some other obvious sore spot or raw nerve. Round off your performance by drinking a toast to Margaret Thatcher and death to all Argies, and – assuming you're still in one piece – step down and join in the bunfight which by now should be well under way on the night-club floor.

Hotel or football stadium demolition. A vital activity, not to be left for those rare occasions when you can pop across the Channel for a football international or for your even rarer World Cup all-in-one package holiday, but ideally an integral part of every Continental excursion. There's nothing that Hitler could do with a couple of Panzer Divisions that you and the lads can't tackle comfortably with your bare hands – so get out there and prove it.

Making an exhibition of yourself on waterskis. Everybody does this when they're learning, but in your case it's different: you go on falling in time after time after time and never get any better at it. This should be enough to convince spectators on the beach that you're a Wally, but if not, try waterskiing while fully clothed, wearing a silly hat or while drinking from a can of Tuborg.

Shopping for souvenirs. Buying trinkets and mementos on the Continent is easy in the sense that in many foreign resorts there's very little else you can buy, but tricky in that it often requires large amounts of money and gullibility. When buying a picture of a little Neapolitan boy with a tear rolling down his cheek or a souvenir-of-Brussels corkscrew you sometimes find yourself being asked to believe that they're the work of local craftsmen – and to pay accordingly.

Caravanning

If you want to spend a Wally fortnight in the British Isles, you couldn't do better than to take a caravan holiday.

One of the great attractions of caravanning is the freedom it gives you. With a 'van' snaking around dangerously behind your car and the open road ahead of you, you're no longer tied down to busy resorts where thousands sit packed like sardines and the stretcher parties can hardly fight their way through the crowds to remove the sunstroke victims. You can go where you like, free as a bird – *and yet still be a Wally.*

This is because caravanning imposes on you an intrinsically Wally life-style, whether you're in splendid isolation in the Peak District or surrounded by endless rows of mobile homes overlooking a gravel pit somewhere in the Thames Valley.

When caravanning, you *have* to eat off Melamine picnic ware and park your bottom on gaily decorated tubular aluminium picnic chairs; you *have* to venture into dark and smelly campsite washrooms, having first made an epic journey past miles of other caravans full of jeering holidaymakers while nervously clutching a torch, a roll of

Andrex and a plastic sponge bag. You *have* to hang Airwicks everywhere to dispel that lingering aroma of fried sausage and Elsan, and drink lukewarm ready-mixed gin and tonic or whisky and ginger ale from screw-top bottles You have to do these things because there is no other way to do them when living in a caravan. Just as there is no such thing as a conservatively dressed limbo dancer or an Indian restaurant with no red-flock wallpaper, so there is no such thing as a non-Wally caravan. You are halfway to being a Wally the moment you step inside one.

But *only* halfway. In order to go the full distance, you must bear in mind the following points:

1) The optimum size for a Wally caravan is always 'too small'. So if you buy one that's not much bigger than a tin of Old Holborn to begin with, you start with an advantage. If on the other hand you go for one of the more opulent and spacious models, it's vital to give it that 'no room to swing a cat' feeling by cluttering it up with colour televisions, ghetto blasters, microwave ovens, and sandwich toasters, even possibly by aralditing a few ornamental knick-knacks in position in or around the window ledges.

2) All genuinely Wally caravans have frilly net curtains or dress drapes in the windows.

3) All genuinely Wally caravans are pitched in the corner of the field or campsite reserved exclusively for Wallies. *I.e.*, the one where other campers or caravanners are in the habit of emptying their tea-leaves, orange peel and slops.

4) All genuinely Wally caravanners belong to the Caravan Club – but not all Caravan Club members are Wallies. However, you do *have* to be a Wally in order to thrill to the prospect of spending a weekend with total strangers on a caravan site somewhere on the outskirts of Birmingham discussing towbars, awnings and the latest developments in the technology of the chemical toilet.

In order to be a genuine Wally caravanner you must not

make the mistake of looking on your caravanning holiday as an opportunity for rest and relaxation in peaceful surroundings. It is nothing of the sort. Essentially, it is a chance to practise being a Wally householder, only in more cramped, uncomfortable and therefore challenging conditions. Your morning routine should be gruelling: getting dressed, converting the sleeping area to the eating area by folding away the bedding and erecting the stow-away table, eating breakfast, washing up, shaking out the rugs and cushions, fetching water and emptying the you-know-whats and returning all the cutlery and cooking utensils to their proper place in cunningly concealed drawers and hidden cupboards ...

If you follow roughly the same procedure in the afternoon and evening, you should find that you're left with virtually no time at all in which to relax and enjoy yourself, but if you do find you have a spare moment, the correct thing to do is to remove yourself from the scene altogether by lifting up one of the seats, climbing into the coffin-like recess below, closing the lid down on top of you and staying there in a Dracula pose with your hands across your chest until it's time to get out and prepare the next meal.

WHERE TO FIND THOSE HOLIDAY TRAFFIC JAMS

For holiday-makers in the British Isles, finding those queues of holiday traffic used to be a hit-and-miss affair. Sometimes you could strike lucky and find yourself slap-bang in the middle of a ten-mile tailback, other times it was plain sailing all the way and you just had to be content with causing a traffic jam of your own. Now, thanks to this easy-to-follow guide, you can plan your route so as to take in the very best of Britain's traffic trouble spots and 'pinch points'.

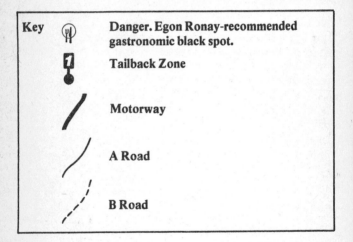

Key		
	🍴	Danger. Egon Ronay-recommended gastronomic black spot.
	1	Tailback Zone
		Motorway
		A Road
		B Road

Thanks to a sudden shortage of motorway where the M6 fizzles out at Carlisle you have to crawl along at a snail's pace all the way to the ferry at Stranraer and probably miss your boat. Ideal for the family Wally.

The A65 between Leeds and the M6 – notorious.

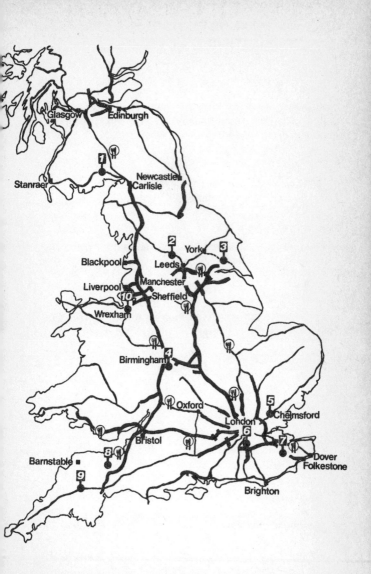

3

● The A1079 between the Humber Road Bridge and York is worth a visit. Market Weighton will be by-passed in 1986 so enjoy the delays while you can.

4

● A missing motorway link between the M5 and M42 south-east of Birmingham creates all-the-year-round carve-ups.

5

● X-certificate hold-ups at Chelmsford as you steam out of London bound for the East Coast holiday resorts.

6

● Picturesque scenes as holiday and commercial traffic from Brighton and Newhaven disgorges into Coulsdon and Purley.

7

● A classic bottleneck as motorway traffic from Dover and Folkestone converges on the old A20 trunk road.

8

● For mile-long queues in beautiful surroundings, try this popular stretch of the A361 from the M5 to Barnstaple.

9

● Explore grockle country on the superbly congested A30 via Okehampton.

10

● The spectacular A483 from Chester to Wrexham makes an ideal holiday route to North Wales for orange-peel and sandwich droppers from Liverpool and Manchester.

HOW TO BE A WALLY AT WORK

Some people are lucky. They have jobs that specifically require them to be Wallies. Door to door double-glazing salesmen, for example. Secondhand car dealers. Local radio disc jockeys. The Lionel Blair Dancers. The Game For A Laugh team. People who sell battery-operated yipping dogs on the pavement in Oxford Street or appear in commercials for Barratt's Homes.

Others are lucky too. Though not contractually bound to be Wallies, they at least have jobs that enable them to dress up in funny clothes and go around looking like Wallies: traffic wardens; Mormons; Butlin's Redcoats; or people who shovel chips into paper bags at Macdonalds or Kentuckies.

But the vast majority are less fortunate. For them, work offers very little opportunity either to behave like a Wally or even to look like one. They have to content themselves with being weekend or spare-time Wallies – or else somehow try and do a job and be a Wally simultaneously.

In practice, combining both is extremely difficult. The problem is, of course, that being a Wally is more than just arduous and time-consuming – *it's a full-time job in itself* (see Job Description, pp. 108-9).

If you doubt this, consider the plight of Wally Post Office clerks. Many of them are so busy being Wallies that they can barely spare the time to issue stamps and television licences. Or take the case of the hard-pressed Wallies who deal with Passenger Enquiries for British Rail. Usually they're so rushed off their feet being Wallies that it takes them a good five minutes before they can get round to answering the phone – and very often they are still busy being Wallies when they do.

As a beginner, your first step towards becoming a Wally at work is to be realistic about what you can and can't achieve. Don't be too ambitious at the outset. In fact, don't be ambitious at all. You'll have quite enough on your plate

Position: Full-time Resident Wally (ungraded)

1. Position of job

   To liaise with other Wallies within the office
   or department and externally regarding the
   previous evening's telly, the prospect of
   Millwall being relegated to the Fourth Division
   the lamentable decline in the quality of the
   chips in the staff canteen, and to adjudicate
   in such matters as which female member of
   staff sports the largest pair of knockers.
   To organise the procurement of giant-size
   birthday cards for other members of staff
   and to inscribe them with obscene limericks
   or snatches of self-penned doggerel. To
   score own goals for the office football
   team and sit on ground for minutes afterwards holding head in hands. To slag off
   and badmouth superiors. To conduct campaigns
   of sexual harassment against secretaries
   and receptionists. To sunbathe in the
   office car park. To ensure that the air is
   at all times heavily laden with the rich
   aroma of sweaty armpits, nylon or polyester
   shirts, bad breath and Player's No. 6. To
   be last out of the building during fire
   drills. To generally promote the spread of
   the British Disease.

2. Position within organisation

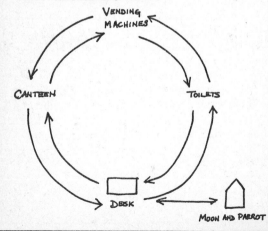

108

3. Functional relationships/contacts

Internal	External
Members of the office squash league, darts team, or magazine circle. Other Dolly Parton fans. Other Capri drivers People selling LPs, Videos, or cut-price tickets for Evita via staff noticeboard.	The Speaking Clock Dial A Disc Cricketline Total strangers who phone up out of the blue for confidential chats about personal finance

4. Additional duties

a) Perform strip-tease on top of filing cabinet during office Christmas party.
b) Get accidentally separated from rest of party during Staff Association coach trip to Munich beer festival.
c) Provide light show and disco for annual company dinner.
d) Go on the rampage during sales conferences, setting off fire extinguishers and destroying hotel furniture.
e) Conduct interesting culinary experiments in the canteen by heaping all the leftovers onto one plate, adding custard and salad cream and stirring to a thick paste.
f) Perpetrate vile smells in the toilets.
g) To be permanently sozzled during exhibitions and trade fairs and wear lapel badge upside down.

Meetings attended

Informal think-tank cum creative barnstorming session in saloon bar of Moon and Parrot (most lunchtimes).
Occassional Gin Rummy school in Post Room on Friday afternoons.

Job holder's Approval *A. Wally*

simply trying to combine being a Wally and being an office junior. Being a Wally and a Captain of Industry comes later. Certainly it calls for skills beyond the scope of a book like this.

The Wally Desk Kit

You cannot hope to discharge your duties as a Wally efficiently unless you have all the necessary equipment to hand. If you work in an office, this means staking out your own little corner of the corporate battlefield and littering it with the following essential aids to executive time-wasting:

1) Notices saying

    Quick! Look Busy. Here comes the Boss!

    The impossible we can do today. Miracles take a little longer.

    You don't have to be mad to work here – but it helps!

    As soon as I can spare the time I'm going to have a nervous breakdown. I've worked for it. I deserve it. No one's going to stop me!

    Why is there always so much month left at the end of the money?

    Wake up with a smile on your face. Sleep with a coathanger in your mouth.

    The world is full of willing people. Some willing to work. Others willing to let them.

    A clean desk is the sign of a sick mind.

    Tomorrow we are going to get organised.

    Laurel and Hardy could do it better!

    Keep smiling – the boss loves idiots.

2) Postcards, preferably dirty ones, from approved Wally holiday resorts.

3) Mascots, rosettes, cuddly toys, team photos and travel posters.

4) Novelty biros, a plastic zip-up pencil case in the form of a giant pencil, a giant plastic comb, a Snoopy pencil sharpener.

5) At least one plastic or paper cup from the office vending machine containing half an inch of cold tea or coffee with a fag-end floating in it.
6) A perspex photo cube containing risque snaps of your uproarious Club Wally holiday in Aghios Nikolaos or Mykonos.
7) An impenetrable sight-screen consisting of rubber plants, Busy Lizzies, maidenhair ferns and castor oil plants, all with fags stubbed out around the base, and liberally watered with vending-machine Bovril.
8) And in the drawers of your desk: squash balls, your very own ping pong bat, a sweatband, Baby Bio, Muscleman Protein Plus Tablets, and huge volumes of awkward correspondence, memos you're sitting on until you can find a way of quietly disposing of them or smuggling them out of the office without anybody noticing.

Planning your day

One of the many frustrating experiences you'll encounter as a Wally in the office is to be sitting quietly at your desk among the fluffy toys and novelties, putting the finishing touches to your prototype for a vertical take-off paper dart, when to your intense annoyance you're suddenly disturbed by a telephone call on some trifling matter from a customer, supplier or member of the public, or by an urgent request from your boss to drop everything and get on to so-and-so in the Accounts department, file an important batch of paperclips, or, more usually, to investigate the non-appearance of his 40 Capstan Full Strengths and mid-morning bacon roll. Given your crowded schedule, this is exactly the kind of distraction you could do without. But how do you avoid it?

You can't, unfortunately. But you can minimise the inconvenience.

One solution is to try to plan ahead, sorting your various tasks into a properly graded list of priorities, so that when the unexpected crisis does crop up and you have no alternative but to get your finger out, you can still plan around it and salvage something from the day. For example, perhaps on this particular occasion you could cut short your usual three-hour stint propping up the bar at the Moon and Parrot at lunchtime and finish the paper dart then. Or you could shelve the project for the meantime and instead try making a Mickey Mouse out of Blue-Tac or removing the crust on your Tippex, or turn your attention to something less labour-intensive, such as nobbling the office vending machine or simply walking up and down on the nylon floor carpet giving people electric shocks.

Of course, it's not always possible to do this. You can't do everything. There are, after all, only so many hours in the day and you have even fewer than most because as a Wally you work to a personal Flexitime scheme which involves being last into the office in the morning and first out at knocking off time. Sometimes you simply have to explain to people that they'll have to wait and that you're fully occupied filling in a questionnaire in *Penthouse* to find out your sexual I.Q. Not in so many words, of course, but by using one of the following time-honoured phrases:

'More than my job's worth ...'
'Not my pigeon ...'
'Up to my eyeballs ...'
'Just a cog in a wheel ...'
'Only one pair of hands ...'

Alternatively, you can send them a letter or memo thanking them for bringing the matter to your notice and assuring them that it is now receiving your most urgent attention.

How to be an executive Wally

No matter how hard you try and avoid it, if you work in any kind of organisation the chances are that sooner or later you're going to get promoted. Usually this is through no fault of your own – just a case of poor judgement on the part of superiors or dead men's shoes.

Often your promotion comes just at a time when you're beginning to get the hang of being a Wally office junior – and it's an undeniable blow. But there are compensations. For a start, life on the lower rungs of the management ladder doesn't necessarily mean more work and less time to be a Wally – often quite the opposite. Secondly, although it does require you to clean up your act somewhat, the changes are cosmetic rather than functional.

Being an executive Wally means no more Male Chauvinist Pig ties and polyester shirts with racing cars dotted all over them. Instead you sport blue stripey shirts with white collars and snazzy three-piece suits from Harry Fenton with jackets that you hang from a little hook behind the driving seat of your company car. Your entire personal appearance becomes smarter, better-groomed. You affect huge gold sovereign ring mounts and a Kevin Keegan hairdo which you pat and preen constantly and check nervously in shop windows; you carry a slim attaché case containing top-secret Kleenex tissues and confidential battery shaver. You no longer pinch bottoms or sneak glances up secretaries' skirts on the stairs; instead you wine and dine them at alcove tables in Italian restaurants and restrict yourself to a furtive grope over the Zabaglione. You no longer pollute the entire department with No. 6 smoke; you've switched to Silk Cut with the odd Slim Panatella – and anyway, you now have an office of your own where you can cough and splutter to your heart's content. As an executive Wally you are more fastidious in matters of personal hygeine too. Where you once emitted ray-gun bursts of raw onion after ploughman's lunches at the Moon and Parrot, you now exude the faintest tang of expense-account garlic mushroom laced with Tic Tac, Polo Mint or Gold Spot. And you no longer smell of armpits and Brut, you smell of Hai-Karate.

As an executive Wally your desk kit, too, is restrained by comparison with your Wally underlings. No profusion of placards, football colours or travel posters here; instead, just a Newton's Cradle, a photo of the wife and kids, and – to show that underneath it all nothing has *really* changed – a plummeting sales graph.

HOW TO BE A SUPERWALLY

What is a Superwally?

A Superwally is someone who drives a Porsche with a sticker in the rear window that says 'My Other Car's A Porsche'. He has mirror-glass installed in his office the wrong way round. He builds a Californian conversation pit in his ranch-style residence in Surrey even though he has nothing to converse about.

A Superwally is someone who keeps a gold-plated personalised pocket calculator cum alarm clock in the breast pocket of his monogrammed silk pyjamas so that he can be woken up in the mornings by an electronic version of the James Bond theme.

Above all, a Superwally is someone whose idea of travelling incognito consists of riding around in a Rolls Royce Silver Cloud with personalised numberplate flanked by motorcycle outriders and police escort – but with his dark glasses on.

How do you become a Superwally? Frankly, your chances are almost nil. You certainly won't do it by hard work, or by taking a correspondence course in business studies, or by following the kind of advice that can be given in a book such as this. You can only become a Superwally by a unique combination of 99 per cent luck, and 1 per cent naked greed and opportunism.

The approved methods are as follows:

1) Getting in at the start of a £100 chain letter
2) Taking part in a Key Markets Scratch Away lottery
3) Winning a contract to supply fruit machines and video games to one of the oil states
4) Accidentally discovering that it is possible to make a commercially viable sausage out of reconstituted kangaroo meat and polystyrene ceiling tiles and proceeding to make a killing in the junk food business.

A Superwally, then, is a Wally who has struck it rich. But curiously, although all Wallies dream of one day breaking into the Superwally bracket, life as a Superwally is no bed of roses. On the contrary, it's extremely hard work – as you may begin to understand if for a moment you put yourself in the shoes of that get-rich-quick sausage king …

Naturally your first step on acquiring your new-found wealth is to sell everything you own and move to a sprawling hacienda near Basingstoke complete with heliport and swimming pool especially built to your own design in the shape of a sausage. And that's when the trouble starts. Immediately news breaks that you've hit the big time, you find yourself being sponged upon by relatives, ripped off by supposed well-wishers and secretly resented by all and sundry. Your nearest neighbours in the mock-Tudor stud farm half a mile away make a point of not inviting you to their drinks parties. You're shunned at the tennis club. Worst of all, your family life beings to suffer. The wife moans and groans constantly about all the extra housework she's expected to do in your spanking new residence. You try and placate her by employing a team of Filipino servants to help out around the home, but it doesn't do any good; all she does now is complain they're nicking the silver – which indeed they are. Your kids too hate you for uprooting them from their old school and packing them off to a private establishment half a mile down a winding gravel drive somewhere in Ascot where they're forced to rub shoulders with a toffee-nosed collection of Jeremies, Jameses, and sons of High Commissioners and African potentates.

And as for *your* social life, on the rare occasions when you do get a chance to chew the fat with your old Wally pals, they seem less interested in talking over old times than in breaking bits off your furniture and removing your personal effects to take back and raffle in the pub.

Under the mounting pressure, you begin to hit the bottle in a big way. The wife, worried by your drinking and worn to a frazzle by more angry scenes with the Filipinos, votes with her feet and goes to stay with her mother in her mobile home in Worthing, leaving you to soldier on as best you can without her.

Plagued by visits from the Inland Revenue and by lurking

suspicions that your accountant is robbing you blind, your thoughts turn nostalgically to days gone by – days when you could spend a carefree evening chucking beer over the lads back at the Moon and Parrot and not have to stand drinks all round the moment you set foot inside the door. Haunted by bittersweet memories, you make a sentimental journey back to the pub you once knew and loved. But more disappointments are in store for you. The Moon and Parrot has vanished, its place taken by a giant hypermarket selling, amongst other things, the vile kangaroo and polystyrene sausages which you now curse yourself for ever having foisted on a gullible world. Sick at heart you return home to Southfork II and in a blind fury of wanton destruction tear the antique brass ornamental telephone out of its socket and put the boot into the wife's collection of Barry Manilow cassettes.

And now, on top of all the domestic grief and the boozing, financial problems begin to loom. On the advice of one of your Superwally friends you invest unwisely and lose your shirt on an abortive scheme for a night-club, casino and time-share apartment complex on a site adjoining the government weapons research establishment on Foulness. The debts begin to pile up. The months of high living – the lavish parties, the wrecked hotel rooms, the pranged limos and Aston Martins, the costly attempts to buy your eldest daughter a starring role in the latest Tim Rice-Andrew Lloyd Webber musical – all take their toll. And bit by bit the fairy tale fortune you amassed by a mixture of luck and sharp dealing in the sausage trade gets whittled away, until all you have left is a private hoard of Krugerrands which you're desperately trying to hide from the taxman.

Finally disaster strikes. Staggering down to breakfast in your towelling robe having demolished an entire bottle of banana liqueur with your early morning cup of tea, you find that a letter has been placed discreetly beside your usual pick-me-up of beaten egg, wheatgerm, brandy and Worcester Sauce by Bruno, your faithful eight-foot-tall deaf-mute manservant and minder.

With trembling fingers you tear open the envelope – but you already know in your heart that it contains dire news.

Sure enough. It's from your accountant, gloatingly informing you that he has absconded to Marbella taking with him not only the ravishing personal assistant and masseuse who was your only comfort over the last harrowing few months, but the entire contents of your wall safe.

Your life is in ruins. Or rather, it *would* be, were it not for one mysterious aspect of the Superwally phenomenon, namely that simply by being a Superwally you are an object of endless fascination to countless thousands of ordinary run-of-the-mill Wallies up and down the country.

Which explains why, just as you are taking a fond leave of Bruno and the Dobermans and preparing to take a farewell dip in your sausage-shaped swimming pool, one of the tabloids phones up out of the blue, offering half a million for the exclusive inside story of your marriage break-up, your heroic battle with the booze and your disastrous business ventures – and the whole grisly circus starts all over again ...

Moral: it may be tough where *you* are, down in the foothills of Wallydom, but it's even tougher for the Superwallies at the top.

Important Dates in the Wally Year

1st January	First hangover of the year
5th January	300 shopping days to Christmas
1st March	Last chance to consume pre-Christmas Lyons Apple and Blackcurrant Sundaes
27th March	Forget to put clocks forward
1st April	Out with the laxative tea bags, Whoopee cushions, onion chewing gum and strap-on rubber boobs
8th April	Buy new shirt in Spring Sale at C & A
9th April	Lose it on Grand National
2nd May	200 shopping days to Christmas
27th August	Bank Holiday. Load up motor with ghetto blaster, metal detector, roadside picnic kit and surfboard and head off to South Coast for the day …
28th August	… forgetting that thousands of other Wallies have had exactly the same idea
30th August	100 Shopping days to Christmas
23rd October	Forget to put clocks back
1st November	Put up Christmas decorations
14th December	Official start of Random Breath Test season
24th December	Christmas Eve. Tear round shops in blind panic trying to buy all presents and provisions in last two hours of trading
25th December	Break ice on Serpentine
26th December	Pitch tent outside Selfridges
31st December	Plunge into Trafalgar Square fountains wearing plastic motorway cone on your head

1. *Grandad* Clive Dunn
2. *There's No One Quite Like Grandma*
   St Winifred's School Choir
3. *Wombling Free* The Wombles
4. *Captain Beaky and his Band* Keith Michell
5. *Do you Think I'm Sexy* Rod Stewart
6. *Happiness* Ken Dodd
7. *The Deck of Cards* Max Bygraves
8. *Two Little Boys* Rolf Harris
9. *Making Your Mind Up* Bucks Fizz
10. *Perhaps Love* John Denver and Placido Domingo
11. *Save Your Love* Renee and Renato
12. *I Write the Songs that Make the Young Girls Cry*
    Barry Manilow
13. *Island in the Sun* Demis Roussos
14. *Viva Espana* Sylvia
15. *Superstar* Karen Carpenter
16. *Puppy Love* Donny Osmond
17. *Tie a Yellow Ribbon Round The Old Oak Tree*
    Dawn
18. *Hooked on Classics*
    The London Symphony Orchestra
19. *Fly The Flag* The 1982 England World Cup Squad
20. *The Birdy Song* The Tweets

Not all great smells come out of green plastic bottles in your bathroom cupboard. Don't miss the great smell of ...

The changing rooms of the Tottenham Court Road Y.M.C.A.
A hot day in Dolcis (shoe shop)
A warm summer's evening on the Kingston By-Pass
Burning clutch fluid
A long-distance lorry driver's sleeping bag
A roadie's singlet
A docker's armpit
Gillette Foamy Lemon and Lime Shaving Cream
A bouncer's shirtfront
Listerine Antiseptic Mouthwash
Scampi in the basket
Radian Warm-Up Sports Rub
Lavender air freshener and fried onions
Boiled fish and cabbage water
Low tide in the Bristol Channel
Midnight in Grimsby
The rear seats of the overnight coach to Glasgow
Tightly packed headbangers at a Status Quo gig

Wally Worldbeaters

A selection from The Wally Book of Records

The supermarket trolley found furthest from its supermarket of origin. Easily the world's most adventurous and well-travelled supermarket trolley is one originally belonging to the Dagenham Finefare fleet. It was hi-jacked by Wallies and later dumped among a container-load of washing-machine spare parts bound for Bahrain.

The longest Conga ever formed by Wallies at an office party. This record is at present held by the Staff Association of the National Westminster Bank who at their annual Xmas knees-up in 1982 managed to form a jubilant singing and dancing human chain consisting of over 3,000 staff members and occupying several floors of the Nat West building in London's Barbican. Eventually the Conga had to be broken up by police using riot shields, batons and water cannon.

The most outstanding contribution by a Wally to safe rail travel. This honour belongs to the unknown Wally in the British Rail design department responsible for devising the famous Inter-City hammer. This object, which has baffled thousands of commuters, can be found beside the window in every Inter-City rail-car and is clearly intended to be used by passengers in the event of a derailment to smash the windows and crawl out to safety. By a stroke of genius, the designer failed to provide any means of removing it from its glass case.

The least famous or noteworthy Wally ever to fit smoked glass windows on his Mini Clubman. Unfortunately the present record-holder is so obscure and ordinary that his name and career details aren't known.

Pam Ayres	Dave Lee Travis
Sue Barker	Liberace
Tony Blackburn	Little and Large
Lionel Blair	Barry Manilow
Katie Boyle	John McEnroe
Rhodes Boyson	Bob Monkhouse
James Burke	Olivia Newton John
Billy Carter	Des O'Connor
Barbara Cartland	The Osmonds
Richard Clayderman	Nicholas Parsons
Brian Clough	Peter Powell
David Coleman	Victoria Principal
Perry Como	Esther Rantzen
Robin Cousins	Robin Ray
Paul Daniels	Ronald and Nancy Reagan
Val Doonican	Kenneth Robinson
Cyril Fletcher	Erica Roe
Bruce Forsyth	Demis Roussos
Gary Glitter	Telly Savalas
Larry Grayson	Barry Sheene
Benny Hill	David Soul
Fred Housego	Arianna Stassinopoulos
Englebert Humperdinck	Rod Stewart
Instant Sunshine	Janet Street Porter
David Jacobs	Denis Thatcher
Tom Jones	John Travolta
Kevin Keegan	Sir Hugh Trevor Roper
Eddie Kidd	David Vine
Evil Knievel	Eddie Waring
Jonathan King	Barbara Woodhouse
The Kings Singers	Jimmy Young
Bonnie Langford	Lena Zavaroni

The Wally Guide to Party Pranks

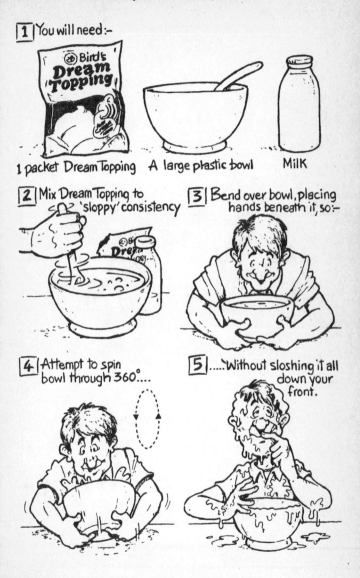

1 You will need :-

1 packet Dream Topping   A large plastic bowl   Milk

2 Mix Dream Topping to 'sloppy' consistency

3 Bend over bowl, placing hands beneath it, so:-

4 Attempt to spin bowl through 360°....

5 .....Without sloshing it all down your front.

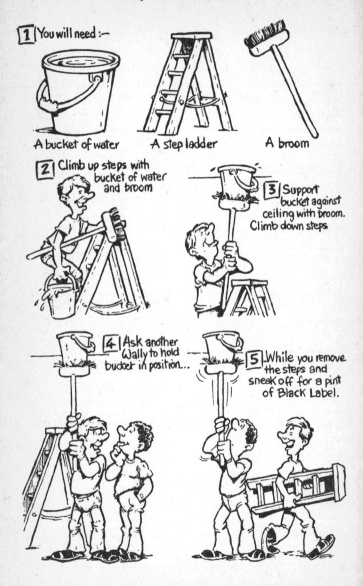

So you think you've got what it takes to be a Wally? Then why not join the All England Wally Club and take part in some of the exciting activities the Club has lined up for the coming year? A mass 'brew-up' outside the Department of the Environment as part of the Club's ongoing campaign for the legalisation of motorway picnicking. A coach excursion, available at specially reduced rates to Club members, to see the spectacular 'Son et Lumière Milton Keynes'. And not forgetting the Annual All England Wally Club Dinner in the car park of the National Exhibition Centre, Birmingham!

To apply for membership, simply study the form below then scribble *ET Phone Home* all over it and deface it exactly as you would a poster on the underground or any piece of time-wasting official-looking bumph.

I hereby declare that having taken on board all the advice contained in this lifesaver of a book I am now a fully fledged Wally. I agree to abide by the rules of the club although I understand that so far the committee have been too busy decorating the Club Headquarters with notices saying 'You don't have to be mad to work here but it helps' actually to get it together to write any. I enclose a cheque for £499.99, which I hope will cover everything.

The All England Wally Club Annual Dinner

I have a pretty good idea what's going to be on the menu of this year's dinner and I have decided:

- ☐ I'll risk it

- ☐ I'd rather be Hemeling

- ☐ I'd be better off at a Berni

Name ....

Address ....

All Futura Books are available at your bookshop or newsagent, or can be ordered from the following address:
Futura Books, Cash Sales Department,
P.O. Box 11, Falmouth, Cornwall.

Please send cheque or postal order (no currency), and allow 45p for postage and packing for the first book plus 20p for the second book and 14p for each additional book ordered up to a maximum charge of £1.63 in U.K.

Customers in Eire and B.F.P.O. please allow 45p for the first book, 20p for the second book plus 14p per copy for the next 7 books, thereafter 8p per book.

Overseas customers please allow 75p for postage and packing for the first book and 21p per copy for each additional book.